AF578777

In Search of the Supernatural

Peter Travis

Wolfe

10 Earlham Street, London WC2H 9LP

First published 1975 by Wolfe Publishing Limited,

© Peter Travis 1975

SBN 7234 0630 8

Printed and bound by A. Wheaton & Co., Exeter

Acknowledgements

I wish to express my gratitude to all those people who have helped me in my researches, without whose help this book could not have been written.

There are some people who deserve a special mention – namely, the newspaper editors who so kindly inserted my letters asking for information about hauntings, etc.; the librarians and their staffs who went to considerable trouble to furnish me with information; Mr Alfred Mills, secretary of the South Staffordshire Metaphysical Society, who supplied me with names of places reputed to be haunted; Mr Donald McCormick and the publisher of his book *Murder by Witchcraft*, who let me use part of a chapter to supplement one of my stories; Arthur Wright and Cecil Jasper, for letting me have many details about some Shropshire hauntings; and the people with whom I have had so much correspondence.

I am indebted to Miss Margaret Salt who worked so hard in typing the manuscript. Without her invaluable help the writing of this book would have taken a much greater time. My thanks also to Sonia Johnson who typed the first draft.

Mr James Wentworth Day, author of so many books on country life and ghosts, kindly offered to read the manuscript and write a foreword. My thanks for his contribution.

For John Priestman, Tony Crank and John Berrington, three good friends, who have shown an interest in some of the events recorded.

Contents

Foreword

by James Wentworth Day

(Author of *In Search of Ghosts*; *A Ghost Hunter's Game Book*; *Ghosts and Witches*; *H.R.H. Princess Marina, Duchess of Kent*; *The Queen Mother's Family Story*; and many more.)

The interest in ghosts, witchcraft, black magic and other aspects of the supernatural has quickened enormously in the last few years. There are differing causes. An interest in ghosts is a perfectly natural interest since most people either regard them as an agreeable, thrilling or horrifying form of folklore or as the possible key to a genuine form of communication with those who have died. Ghost stories, in fine, are part of the story-teller's magic which has fascinated humanity for untold centuries.

Mr Travis's approach to the subject is that of the story-teller who is at the same time a painstaking researcher with an unshakeable faith in God and the Christian religion. There could be no better approach.

It is utterly different from the morbid, unhealthy curiosity and downright evil which characterises most of the 'with it' dabblers in black magic. They represent not only atheism at its worst but the Forces of Evil. They are either active disciples of the Devil – I am not in the least ashamed of using the old-fashioned phrase – or they are, in too many pathetic cases, half-baked adolescents who have been caught up by this dangerous cult.

Mr Travis's book, therefore, is all the more welcome, since he deals calmly and dispassionately with first-hand or well-founded stories of supernatural happenings. He makes the sharp point that there are definite forces for good and evil in this world and that they affect people decisively.

I, for one, do not doubt for a moment that ghosts exist. At the end of the First World War, as a young soldier, with a companion, I saw in broad daylight a ghostly cavalry skirmish between German Uhlans and French Dragoons at a spot on the Franco-Belgian frontier where, as we subsequently discovered, such skirmishes had occurred between advanced scouting patrols during the Napoleonic wars, the War of 1870 and in 1914. We saw this in broad daylight six weeks after the Armistice was signed.

I could quote other instances of known occurrences of ghosts seen by level-headed people when they least expected to see them. There is, in fact, no reason why ghosts should not make themselves seen for reasons which we do not yet understand. The telling of ghost stories, particularly true ones, is therefore an essential part of national literature. As such, Mr Travis's book will have its deserved niche.

Those, however, who write to extol the cult of black magic with its infinite capacity for obscene and deadly evil are murderers of the soul. They are the enemies of the Christian religion. May I wish Mr Travis's book the success it so richly deserves.

Ingatestone, Essex.

Introduction

Stories with ingredients of the macabre, tales of those long dead who cannot rest, unearthly scenes which have terrified the beholder, and strange happenings, many of which defy explanation; all these will be found in this book, a collection of stories which I hope will take you beyond mere interest.

The supernatural has always been a subject that has evoked, shall we say, a special kind of inquisitiveness, a search for the knowledge that there is life beyond the grave. Many cannot believe that there is a complete cessation of life, but that the soul, the spirit, the personality, call it what you will, lives on and that some of these spirits are yet earthbound, unable, for some inexplicable reasons, to leave the places in which they lived in the physical body.

The question of good and evil is as old as history itself. The contemporary religions of ancient civilisations were in some ways a search for an answer. Gods of evil, whose influence extended to mere mortals, were constantly warring with deities of more virtuous dispositions, but these are now part of historical mythology although they still have considerable interest for the scholar of history and we must not underestimate the effect such beliefs had on a nation's achievements as well as on its downfall.

In the New Testament, St Paul writes about Man fighting against principalities and powers of darkness, as though we can be, and often are, influenced by unseen but potent forces of evil. I do not intend to present a thesis on Good versus Evil. If we so choose, we can be influenced for the good. On the other hand, Man can be used for purposes of such wickedness and barbarism that the mind is revolted by the memories of past atrocities committed by human beings on their fellow men.

Man is compounded of strange and contrasting qualities. He has tremendous potential for good, or evil – I firmly believe that we have the choice. Some are moved to perpetrate acts of violence so horrible that we cannot believe that such sub-human deeds are possible.

But why do men do these things? What terrible powers drive them to such wickedness? The powers of darkness are not to be sneered at, nor should they be tampered with, but we need to be constantly on our guard against their influence.

This book is not an attempt to prove or disprove a theory of life after death – the stories are too varied in content and subject matter for that purpose. But many of the events recorded are too well authenticated to be disregarded as the products of the overworked imaginations of frightened people.

My researches have taken me far and wide and this has enabled me to meet interesting people who have related their stories, many of which are personal experiences. This is by far the most satisfactory method of research, for it has given me the opportunity to thoroughly question those involved and it has placed me in a position where I can, to a large extent, draw my own conclusions. I have also been involved in a considerable amount of correspondence with others whom for various reasons it has been very difficult to meet. Distance and lack of time have made letter writing a necessity. My third form of research, that of looking up old historical documents, books on legends and folklore, is the least satisfying of all, but as some of the stories are at least three hundred years old, there was no other way of finding them. Even this has proved to hold some interest, because comparisons of a story told by two or more different writers have revealed variations in the narrative. Generally speaking, this has added interest rather than reduced it.

I have for some time been interested in psychical research. I have a special kind of inquisitiveness which seeks to know the unknowable. All psychic phenomena cannot be explained by cold, rational facts; there is much that remains unexplained, therefore I undertook the writing of this book partly to help myself in the quest into the unknown.

As a Christian, I believe in life after death, but it seems that there are earthbound spirits abroad, and some manifest themselves from time to time. Since making my investigations I am not much nearer answering the question of why they are earthbound, but I am more convinced that they exist.

I am by nature a preservationist – I don't like change, even though it is inevitable – and there are certain aspects of our heritage that are well worth preserving. The stories which are included in this book I feel fall into that category. I have been greatly surprised by the amount of interest which has been shown in these stories. Many people have written asking me to reserve them a copy of the book.

Whether you are an avid believer in the supernatural or a hardened sceptic, I believe that these stories will make you consider that all supernatural phenomena are not 'bunkum'. My researches have been as thorough as time will allow, and some of the stories leave me in little doubt of the fact that we 'live on'.

Peter Travis,
Newcastle-under-Lyme,
Staffordshire.

Ghostly Footsteps

It is not only the stately homes of England which can claim to have their own particular ghost; smaller houses contain spirits of the past, and there are two in north Staffordshire which I know have poltergeist activity. Ornaments, pictures, cups and saucers and all manner of objects are, from time to time, flung indiscriminately and for no apparent reason all round the house. Sometimes the activity is quite violent, then for months the 'thing' remains dormant, but then rises from its supernatural hibernation with no warning other than a chair hurled across the room or a picture ripped off a wall. These two houses are about a hundred years old and each is one in a row of terraced houses. Exorcism has been attempted in one of them, but without success.

This story concerns poltergeist activity, and the events take place in a small house in a poor quarter of Birmingham. The Hockley district of Birmingham, like most outskirts of large cities, has its poor quarters where conditions leave much to be desired. The age of the house is difficult to determine but the property is very old and has housed a number of families. The narrow streets and long rows of terraced houses give the area a sombre and somewhat depressing atmosphere. In Park Road, Hockley, there stands a house which I am not prepared to disclose, but I have all the details of the place which has quite a history of ghostly happenings; of footsteps and 'things' seen. At the present the place is not inhabited, nor is it likely to be, for it is to be demolished and at the time of going to press this may well have taken place.

Mr Dennis Jones was born there in 1935. His mother and father moved into the house in 1926 and when Mr Jones was only a child he can distinctly remember his parents speaking about strange noises and 'happenings' that took place in the house, although he himself had not seen or heard anything unusual – that is, until he was fourteen years old.

He had been left alone in the house one afternoon when the handle of the door which opened on to steps leading down into the cellar began to rattle violently – this went on for a few seconds and not surprisingly the boy was very startled. Outside the house, and placed immediately in front of the door, was a coal grate, but this was always firmly secured from the inside of the cellar by a chain. The boy's first reaction was to think that someone had got into the cellar and was attempting to burgle the house. He ran out into the street. There was no one about and he discovered that the coal grate was still firmly fastened by the chain. Of course someone could have climbed down if the chain had not been attached to the grate and then secured it once they were in the cellar.

When his parents returned he told them of his frightening experience but they put it down to his imagination, yet he was aware that his parents glanced at each other with a knowing look. Investigations of the cellar, as expected, revealed that no one had been there, at least they had not entered from outside.

From that time onwards noises were heard with greater frequency and the explanation given was that of the old age of the house. Old houses, his parents said, were bound to have creaking boards and places where draughts blew, but Mr Jones was not entirely satisfied with these statements. There was more to it than that. It was as if they were not reasons at all, but excuses for something that his parents were trying to cover up.

About 1958, Mr Jones's mother became ill and she usually retired to bed by half past nine at night, sometimes earlier, leaving Mr Jones and his father downstairs by themselves. The room in which they sat was directly under the bedroom in which the sick woman lay and it was at this time that strange noises were heard in the bedroom. At first it was thought the noise was caused by Mrs Jones having to get out of bed. Footsteps were heard walking across the room. The son, on one occasion, thinking his mother was in need of help, ran up the stairs to see what was the matter; to his surprise she was sound asleep!

Night after night the footsteps were heard, at about the same time every night, and walking in the same direction. Each time the father or the son went upstairs to see what was going on they discovered Mrs Jones asleep. The footsteps could be heard at half past ten every night and they walked from the door in the righthand corner of the room in a diagonal approach to the far left-hand corner.

In 1964 Mr Jones's mother died. Before her death Mr Jones had married and left the house, living in a flat with his wife. After Mrs Jones's death her son and his wife returned to the house to live with Mr Jones senior. They had been in the house for only a fortnight when Mrs Jones remarked that she had a feeling that she was being watched. She had not heard of the strange noises in this house, so therefore she was unaware of its past history as experienced by her husband and his parents.

She said that she never felt alone in the house, as if there was an unseen presence always there. One Sunday afternoon she was in the bedroom, which was the one in which Mrs Jones senior had slept, when the door opened by itself. Now the latch on this door was a particularly difficult one to move and sometimes it took considerable effort to open the door. As the door opened Mrs Jones looked up and to her surprise she saw what she described as a black shadow.

The shape was about five feet in height and noiselessly moved across the room from the door to the opposite corner – it took the same route as the footsteps had taken some time ago. Mrs Jones was startled, but she had no feeling of fear.

After this event, the activities of the 'thing' increased, footsteps were heard quite audibly and with almost clockwork regularity. Then other things began to happen. The television would be switched off by an unseen hand, lights would go on and off and the clicking of the switch could be distinctly heard, but yet no one felt afraid.

In 1967 Mr Jones senior died and the young couple left the house. The place was not empty for long, for a family soon moved in, but then things really began to happen. The woman was foul-mouthed and the husband a drunken layabout. Pots and pans were thrown around the rooms as if by their own volition, furniture was upturned on its own accord, doors opened and slammed shut with alarming violence. It was as if the presence resented the way of life of these new residents. They only stayed a few weeks, their experiences in the house were too much for them – their nerves were almost shattered.

It is interesting to note that while the Jones family lived in the house there was no fear of the 'presence', nor were they alarmed at the ghostly and unaccountable footsteps, even after the death of Mrs Jones when the 'activities' became more frequent.

I have tried to discover a little more concerning the history of the place, that is, before 1926, but results have proved negative. Perhaps there had been a tragedy in the house, or was it that some previous occupant was so happy there that even after death it could not leave? The answer will never be known, but one thing is certain, there seemed to be no malevolence connected with the spirit, except when the Jones family left – then events really took a turn for the worse. A strange story, but a fascinating one.

Birmingham

Harbinger of Death

Some houses have a distinct atmosphere of evil and a few people I have interviewed have told me that they have believed they have been in the presence of some evil force; an overwhelming sensation which evokes fear. This kind of sensation is not always felt in old houses, although it is more common in such places. New houses, where there is no history of tragedy, are known to emanate such fear, but of course, this is not to say that a tragedy of some kind did not occur in the area before the house was built and has been unrecorded.

This story might well have something to do with an historic tragedy which did not happen in the house about which I write, but is the result of something rather horrible that took place a very short distance away when the area was largely rural.

Today Birmingham is a large, sprawling city, its centre teeming with people and humming with activity. On the outskirts of the city and to the north is the district of Handsworth with its large and ancient rambling houses, many of which are now converted into flats. It is in this district that there stands a house with an evil reputation. I shall refer to the person who once lived there and who has given me much information about the place as Mrs C. The house is now empty and boarded up ready for demolition.

We need to go back over forty years, for it was in 1930 that Mrs C moved into a very old house in a part of Handsworth which was not the most salubrious of areas. Houses were scarce and, being recently married and having a baby girl only a few months old, she and her husband were glad to accept this particular accommodation.

The house, one of four, was situated in a large yard. It was damp and full of vermin, a most undesirable residence, but as this house was the only one available and their need was near desperate they had to make do. There had been one large room upstairs but by the time when Mr and Mrs C moved in, it had been divided into two rooms, one of them being considerably smaller than the other. Stairs from the sitting-room led directly to the small bedroom which was at the back of the house.

Right from the beginning both Mrs C and her husband felt that there was a presence in the place, and that the feeling was stronger in a certain part of the house. To quote Mrs C, 'The feeling felt very strong at the top of the stairs and it penetrated both rooms, especially at night.'

They both slept in the larger front bedroom and it was in this room that Mrs C experienced two very unusual and disturbing happenings.

At about three o'clock one morning she was roused from sleep by something moving about the room. She sat up in bed and was aware that the feeling of the presence was very much stronger than at any previous time. By the window she could make out a shape. It was white and although there was no real definite outline it seemed to be tapered, narrow at the top and widening at the bottom. The thing stood there for a few moments and then seemed to float towards the bed. Mrs C was too terrified to shout, in fact she could not have done so had she wished.

The white mist moved to the side of the bed where her husband was soundly sleeping and there it stayed for what seemed endless time. On reflection Mrs C thought that it could have been just for a few seconds. Eventually, and only gradually, the 'thing' melted into the darkness and the feeling of being watched left.

The next day they received news of a tragedy which had taken place in the family. Mr C's nephew, a boy of fourteen, had been discovered drowned. Apparently Mr C was very fond of him and there was a real bond of friendship between the two. Mrs C was also very upset by the tragedy.

What or who was the precursor, and had it come to inform the couple of a death? Even after this frightening episode there was still the feeling of a presence in the house although nothing more was seen, until, that is, a few years later.

Mrs C was sleeping in the same bedroom when she saw the outline of a woman; there was a very definite shape and in her arms she was carrying a small child. The figure moved around the room for some time until it faded. On this occasion Mrs C did not feel afraid of what she saw. There seemed to be a sense of peace in the room, but she was very apprehensive, for she remembered the news that followed the previous vision.

Only a short time after this appearance she received news that her niece had lost her newborn child. Apparently the baby had lived for only a few days. Again, was it a forewarning of death?

Mrs C's daughter strongly believed that there was evil in the house and was not happy living there. When she was alone in the smaller of the two bedrooms she was always aware of some kind of presence. She could not describe it in words. Nothing was seen by her but the feeling was ominous.

It is interesting to note the feelings of Mr C. He too felt that he was never alone in the house. At one period of his life he was confined to bed with an illness and he was absolutely convinced that there was someone, or something, in one corner of the room.

According to Mrs C, the house is about one hundred and forty years old and was at one time a wash-house. Her daughter, even to this day, shudders at the thought of the place – the presence of evil was always there.

Years ago there was a well near the house (this would be at the time when the area was open countryside) and there was rumour that many years ago there was a tragedy connected with it. Certainly, she remembers the story of a suicide in a shop which was only a few yards from the house. She speaks of ill luck all the time they lived there, nothing seemed to go right for them. The fact that the house was in such an awful condition did not help matters, but more than that there was continual ill fortune.

Did the house have an evil influence on their lives? Both mother and daughter were more than glad to leave the place two years after the death of Mr C. The atmosphere depressed and frightened both of them. Precursors of death are not unknown. They come to warn, how and why we may never know – but come they do.

Interventions by the Dead

It is not unknown for the spirits of the departed to intervene in the affairs of the living. I have read about people who claim that supernatural intervention has saved them from death or serious injury. Recently I have been in contact with a person who firmly believed that he had an experience which he felt could only be explained in terms of a supernatural intervention.

He was rather reluctant to give me his story, for he does not wish to be labelled as a crank, yet the more he thought about the experience the more he found it difficult to rationalise.

The man who told me his story was employed as a clerk in a factory near Manchester, but in 1954 he moved to Macclesfield with his wife and children. To make the daily twenty-two mile journey to work he had a cycle which was equipped with a small engine; at that time such a mode of transport was quite popular.

One of his colleagues at the office was a firm believer in the world of the supernatural and told him that the spirit world and the physical world often overlapped and that she herself had conversed with the dead. He was sceptical about such views, but a subsequent experience dispelled any such doubts. His journey home took him through Alderley Edge where there was a nine mile stretch of road on which there were no lights. At one point along the journey home there was a side road, Alderley Cross, and if he turned left there, rather than along the road to the traffic lights at Monks Heath, the route which he normally took, it would be a short cut to Macclesfield. The mileage on the signpost at Alderley Cross indicated that this way home might well take less time. The night he decided to do this was very dark and pouring with rain. He stopped his machine and by lifting the cycle and rotating the front wheel he was able to shine his front light on the signpost.

He also noticed in the beam of his light a man sitting motionless on a bicycle at the entrance to the side road. He walked across to him, but the man slowly cycled away in the direction of Monks Heath. Not feeling absolutely certain that the new route would be a short cut after all, he decided to return home the usual way via the cross-roads at Monks Heath. His cycle was fitted with a small engine and so he could easily have overtaken the man who had cycled away a few seconds earlier, but he saw no sign of him.

The following day he related his experience and his colleague, Mrs C, told him that the figure he had seen at Alderley Cross was leading him away from danger. He scoffed at such an idea and said that to disprove such a ridiculous notion he would return home that night by travelling along the road leading to Macclesfield from Alderley Cross. He was quite convinced that the man he saw was 'flesh and blood' and not a supernatural manifestation.

The night was dark and cloudy but it was fine. There followed a series of happenings which affected his machine. First of all a fault occurred which made his lights flash intermittently. He stopped at a cycle store and replaced the bulbs and checked the wiring. Satisfied that all was now in working order, he continued his journey. He left Alderley Edge where the road was well illuminated and soon came to the stretch where there were no lights, which was like entering a dark and forbidding tunnel as the trees on either side of the road formed an arch.

Eventually he reached Alderley Cross, about half a mile north of Nether Alderley, and took the new road home. Suddenly the engine (49 c.c.) spluttered and became lifeless. He pushed the cycle to the top of the hill, hoping that a downhill start would bring the engine back to life. But before he mounted the machine he noticed that something else was wrong, the chain had worked loose and as it was enclosed in a metal chain-guard there was nothing he could do in the dark. Not to be deterred, he ran the cycle down the hill, jumped on to it and eventually the engine fired. His front light began to flicker and as he leaned over to see if his rear light was functioning properly the machine got out of control. It was gathering speed at an alarming rate and he approached a bend in the road which he failed to negotiate and both man and cycle came to grief.

He found himself lying in the road, dazed and shocked, but

suffering from only minor cuts and bruises. How long he lay there is not really known, but it was probably just for a few seconds. He thought how lucky he had been to avoid serious injury and possibly death when suddenly and without warning a car came hurtling round the bend so quickly that all he could remember was drawing his legs into the side of the road and watching with cold horror the wheel of the car miss his foot by inches. His experience shattered him and he remembers virtually nothing of the remainder of the journey.

The following day Mrs C was waiting at her desk and before he could say a word she said, 'You were in grave danger last night because you did not heed my advice.' It was impossible for her to have known anything about the accident, he had meant to tell her but she knew *before* he mentioned the matter.

This of course is not absolute proof of being able to contact the dead, but it does seem as though Mrs C possessed some quality which enabled her to foretell danger. The figure on the cycle at Alderley Cross remains a mystery, and yet it fits in with Mrs C's forecast. Do the dead come to warn us of impending danger? If they do, then not all are malevolent spirits as some would think.

Another story concerning the dead coming back to warn people takes us much further back into history.

Today Ash Hall is the administration offices of Allied English Potteries Ltd, but during its history it has belonged to various families and business concerns.

On the site where the present building stands there used to be an Elizabethan mansion, but this crumbled to decay and was eventually dismantled in 1841. Soon after this, Job Meigh began to build the present Hall. It is in the Tudor manorial style with attractive oriel windows and commands an impressive view. The stone which was used in the building was quarried on the estate itself and the stone is an ash colour – hence the name of the place.

The last owner occupier was William Meigh who died in 1922 and his wife a year later. Soon afterwards the Hall was sold and converted into a hotel with a nine-hole golf course. Later it became a Country Club and in 1942 it was taken over by the Cassel Hospital, evacuated from Kent. In 1946 it was turned into a hotel once again and in 1952 purchased by a business group. It has been the offices of Allied English Potteries for about eighteen years.

The story of the haunting is concerned with the Elizabethan mansion which was standing before the present building, although the cellars of this previous place can still be seen.

After the death of a former resident named Geoffrey Wood (some accounts give his name as Godfrey Wood) strange noises and lights were to be seen coming from his room.

It appears that the family had kept a dreadful secret and those who knew about it swore not to reveal it to anyone. This particular skeleton in the family cupboard remained a mystery, but through my researches it is possible that it is no longer a secret.

One of the servants at the Hall somehow heard about this secret and was crafty enough to gather together bits of information which, when pieced together, placed in his hands a powerful weapon. He intended selling what he knew to someone who could make use of the information which would ruin the family.

One night, after the death of Geoffrey Wood, his ghost appeared to the lady of the house, warning her of the servant's intentions. Next morning, shocked and agitated, she charged the servant with what amounted to treachery, but as was expected he denied it. A few days later the lady and the servant were out riding. Darkness had already fallen and they were making their way back to the Hall. Behind the building was a bridge which crossed a stream, and it was here that the ghost of Geoffrey Wood appeared a second time. The servant was struck with terror and the apparition denounced him. He confessed his guilt and swore to keep the secret.

Now to the secret itself. I spent a considerable time researching this story and my own conclusion is that one member of the family was a murderer whose crime went undetected.

One owner of the house kept his daughter locked up in one of the rooms because she had formed an attachment with someone her father thought unsuitable and below his daughter's station. It is said that the father killed his daughter's lover and that the girl, on hearing about his terrible fate, tried to commit suicide.

The Hall is built on a piece of levelled ground on a hill. In front of the Hall there is a large forecourt and where this ends there is a steep bank of about seven or eight feet. A passage ran from the back stairs of the Hall under the forecourt to the embankment, and it is said that the young lovers often met secretly in the tunnel, but the affair was discovered by the girl's father who confined his daughter to her room. The fate of the unfortunate lover has already been mentioned. Was this the secret that the family so desperately wanted to keep? No doubt it would have been disastrous for the family if that information ever found its way into the hands of the law.

I visited Ash Hall in 1969 and was given a conducted tour of the place. I was taken down to the cellars and shown the entrance to the tunnel which ran under the forecourt, but today it is bricked up.

No one in recent times has seen the apparition, but of course today there is no one living who could reveal the family secret. The spirit of Geoffrey (Godfrey) Wood rests in peace – or does it? I have my doubts.

Cheshire

The Watcher

It is true to say that some houses have atmosphere, and this is not necessarily because of a particular kind of architecture, or any period in history. I believe that atmospheres in some houses are the result of the lives – and deaths – connected with them. On entering some houses one at once senses a feeling of warmth and contentment. Other houses emanate a coldness which is not physical, but which is depressive, giving the feeling of oppression and a sense of being unwelcome. In some instances this can be associated with events that have taken place within the house even though one may be completely ignorant of its history.

Some people say that they can sense the presence of death, not that which has happened, but a death which is imminent, even though there are no obvious reasons for such fears and they do not know of anyone likely to die – and yet this presentiment often materialises with the death of someone in the house.

I have been in contact with a Mrs W and through considerable correspondence an interesting story has come to light. Before Mrs W was married she and her fiancé, like many young couples, were looking for a place to live. Eventually they found an old house in Sale, Cheshire, which was situated near a very busy main road which led to Manchester. The flat was by no means 'self-contained' but, as Mrs W said, the price was reasonable. The other people who lived in the house seemed to be quite a decent crowd who kept themselves very much to themselves.

They decorated their flat before actually moving in. They stayed in the house just twelve months. Mr and Mrs W's flat was situated on the first floor and when they required fuel for their fire it meant that they had to descend the stairs which led into the spacious cellars.

When they moved out of the flat they were visited by a friend who was at that time living in the old house they had only recently vacated. During the conversation Mr and Mrs W and their friend openly admitted that they had 'feelings' about the place, and that all three of them had these peculiar sensations in exactly the same places in the house.

Mrs W confessed that all the time they lived there she felt that they were being 'watched' by someone or something they would not wish to meet. There was a malevolence and maliciousness about the presence, as though there was impending tragedy. This awareness of evil was more pronounced in certain parts of the building, especially in the cellars and in the bathroom, when the blinds were pulled down in the latter room, yet both these places were quite well lit by electric lights. The landing was also affected and it was at this spot that Mr W had two very unusual experiences.

Mrs W points out that her husband would have scoffed at the idea of ghosts, apparitions, or anything connected with the supernatural, that is, until he moved into this house. One evening between eleven and twelve, while standing outside one of the rooms, he saw a glow which began to form itself into a shape, but soon disappeared. His wife saw nothing at the time. On a second occasion Mr W was ascending the stairs when a faint shape passed him. He stopped immediately and watched the 'thing' glide down the stairs and pass by him. It appeared to have the form of a man and was about five feet in height. There was a sense of evil as it went past. After two or three seconds when it was behind him he turned round, but there was nothing there. All this time the light was on and again the time was somewhere between eleven and twelve at night.

The house, still standing and inhabited, is situated in its own grounds which were very overgrown as the garden was completely neglected. The rear of the house was dark and rather forbidding, but the front part was only a few feet away from the busy main road. Yet despite the close proximity to the road they felt as if they were compelled to hurry through those neglected grounds. There was the fear of being 'jumped on', as if someone was lying in wait.

The person who owned the house also lived there and was, unknown to the rest of the occupants, critically ill. He was a man who was almost a recluse.

There was an elderly lady who lived in a bedsitter on the

ground floor and she knew the landlord quite well. One weekend she left to visit her sister and during her absence Mrs W went downstairs to get some coal and passed quite close to the landlord's door. She thought she heard him cough, which put her mind at rest, because she had seen his bottle of milk and newspaper still in the hall, when by this time it had been usually taken inside his room. The following morning she saw that neither milk nor paper had been collected and this gave her cause for grave concern. Both Mrs W and her husband tried to open his door, but without success. It was locked.

Mrs W made enquiries of the other occupants to see if they knew the whereabouts of the landlord. Perhaps he had gone away, but no one seemed to be able to throw any light on the matter. The following day the elderly lady was due back, so Mrs W took the day off work to await her return. Eventually she arrived and when Mrs W related her story the woman was convinced that the landlord was either seriously ill or even dead.

The police were called in and forced an entry into his room. The man was lying in bed utterly helpless; he had suffered a severe stroke and could not speak. Two days later in hospital he had another stroke and died. A couple of days after his death Mrs W's mother-in-law visited her and immediately she walked over the threshold she said that someone had only very recently died. She was not aware of the landlord's death.

For about a week after his passing, the house literally reeked of death and then quite suddenly the feeling of being watched left the house. It was as though the house was 'satisfied'. Mr and Mrs W moved out shortly after this event and Mrs W admitted that her nerves would not have stood much more of the place – there was evil in that house. All this happened in 1964 and the memories of the place are very vivid in the minds of the Ws.

There is no satisfactory explanation of these events. The Ws are level-headed people; Mr W a very down-to-earth person who sometimes feels that what happened was, perhaps, the result of an overworked imagination, and yet another part of him tells him that the house did have a presence.

Was death playing a waiting game in the house and, if so, why? What were the lights which Mr W saw – supernatural phenomena, a portent of death?

Chingle Hall

February 25th, 1970, was a beautiful day. The sun shone from a cloudless sky and the interior of the car in which I travelled was pleasantly warm. Des McKenna and I sped northwards along the M6 and we talked of only one thing, our all-night vigil in a reputed haunted house not far from Preston.

Only a few days earlier I had completed some written work in which there were accounts of the experiences of others who had come into contact with supernatural phenomena. Now I was embarking on a project that was to involve me personally in the investigation of haunted houses, and, I hoped, lead me to incursions of the paranormal.

Des McKenna had helped me with some stories from Cheshire as I had been unable to afford the time to personally investigate them, and I invited him to join me in an all-night vigil at Chingle Hall.

We left the motorway at junction 32 and travelled along the A6 for a mile and then turned off and made our way to the quaintly named village of Goosnargh. After one or two enquiries we managed to find the whereabouts of this ancient manor house.

Chingle Hall is not a large building, in fact it can be considered small for a manor house, but its antiquity and long association with the Roman Catholic Church have marked it as a place of considerable importance. As recently as April 1962 ecclesiastical history was made when the Roman Catholic Archbishop of Liverpool and the Protestant Bishop of Lancaster met within its walls.

The house is cruciform in shape, white-walled and surrounded by a moat over which is built a stone bridge; the successor to a drawbridge. Passing over this bridge one is brought face to face with a massive, studded oak door, believed to be the original one and therefore over seven hundred years old, for the house was built about 1260 by Adam de Singleton. Hanging on this stout front door is a large and heavy 'Y' knocker which is the only one in the country. The approach to this door is through a porch which has, on its south side, a very interesting feature in the form of a signal window which is about nine inches square and contains the original glass. During the times of the Catholic oppression a light would be placed in the window which indicated to those of the Catholic faith that Mass was secretly being celebrated.

Chingle Hall is the birthplace of the Blessed John Wall, a Franciscan priest who lived and worked near Kidderminster until he was arrested and subsequently executed at Worcester in 1679 and was, therefore, one of the last English Roman Catholic priests to die for his Faith. According to Dom Bede Camm in his book, *Forgotten Shrines*, Chingle Hall passed to the Wall family in 1585 and John Wall was born there in 1620. After his execution, tradition tells us that his head did a grand tour of the Continent. There is another story which tells of how his head was smuggled from Worcester to Chingle Hall and buried in the grounds.

Today many pilgrims from all parts of the country come to the house to pay homage to the martyr. But although long dead, does his spirit still linger? This is what we hoped to discover, and we were not to be disappointed in our stay.

On our arrival we were given a homely welcome by Mrs Howarth, the present owner of the Hall, and her sister Miss Ann Strickland. Within the space of a few minutes we were given a thorough conducted tour of the ground floor and told something about the fascinating history of the place.

There are many interesting features of the interior, not least among which are the priests' hiding holes thought to have been constructed by Nicholas Owen, the famous builder of hiding places in the late sixteenth and early seventeenth centuries.

In one of the rooms downstairs which is immediately to the right of the dining-room there were discovered two things of considerable interest. The room contains a massive beam under which was a modern brick fireplace. This was removed and in the alcove there was found a hiding place measuring three feet by two feet and some two feet six inches deep. Probably vestments and other religious articles would be hidden in it. In 1962 another discovery was made, namely a pre-Reformation 'Praying Cross'. Miss Ann Strickland was knocking old plaster off the wall to the right of the alcove when suddenly large pieces began to fall away revealing an ancient oak cross set in a shallow recess. This room was no doubt used for offering up family prayers and what had been discovered was probably part of the altar.

Upstairs there are a number of rooms, two of which need special mention. The first one is traditionally known as the Chapel or Priest's Room and it contains in one wall what appears to have been a window, for it has three stone mullions and, behind these, four panels of stonework in a recess, as though the lights themselves had been filled in. The stonework, however, is actually part of a wall beyond which is yet another room. This 'window' is thought to have been the place where an altar stood, and may in fact have actually been part of it, because the four recessed panels are sufficiently deep to have supported either statues or candlesticks. On the right-hand side of the false window the plaster has been carefully removed to reveal a wonderful example of wattle and daub and also shows a space in which a man could have found a hiding place and which doubtless once had a concealed entrance.

The adjoining room, which is immediately above the porch, is roughly the same size and plan, and experts suggest that this particular room may well have been the place where John Wall was born. There is an interesting tradition which states that it was here that John Wall was baptised by his fellow-martyr the Blessed Edmund Arrowsmith. It is this room more than any other that has the reputation of being haunted, and this was to be the place where Des McKenna and I were to spend the night although we had Mrs Howarth's permission to visit other rooms in the Hall if we felt it necessary.

After we had been there about an hour the Rural Dean arrived and in a short time we were engrossed in conversation. He was the first of many people I was to interview that night who had experienced unusual and quite inexplicable events at Chingle Hall. The Dean related accounts which he considered to be startling, unaccountable, and yet not frightening.

Some little time ago he was sitting in the lounge, a long, spacious and pleasant room of seventeenth-century character: the room in which we were all sitting. He had finished a meal and was talking to Mrs Howarth about the Hall and its contents when suddenly, and for no apparent reason, two pictures on the wall opposite the fireplace began to rattle violently. Now this is rather odd because there are eight such pictures, all of them grouped near each other, yet only two of them did this strange thing.

It was as though invisible hands had grasped the two pictures and for devilish amusement banged them against the wall. Both the Dean and Mrs Howarth were afraid that the glass might shatter with the violent movement. This lasted for about a minute and as suddenly as it had begun it stopped. For some time the two startled observers were speechless.

I asked the Dean for his comments about the happening and I also asked him if he believed the place to be haunted. He replied that he felt that there was a presence, but it was not in any way malevolent, but just who or what the presence was he could not say. This was the first of many incidents which were reported to us.

After tea we met other people, one of whom was a senior police officer, a rationalist if ever there was one, as the nature of his work demanded facts. It would be unlikely that anything told us by such a person would be the product of his imagination. It appears that Chief Superintendent X had known Chingle Hall for about twelve years and during that time he had paid frequent visits to the place.

A short time after Christmas 1967 the Chief Superintendent and his wife were invited to have dinner at the Hall. The meal over, the guests adjourned to the sitting-room. At approximately a quarter to nine, sounds directly above them were heard, sounds of an unusual kind. There was, first of all, a thump, as though someone had dropped a heavy object on to the floor – then complete silence. Everyone in the sitting-room looked at each other. Again, a distinct thud was heard in exactly the same place. No one was upstairs. All the guests could be accounted for – they were together downstairs, and in that one room. Following these two bumps came the sound of a heavy tread, as though someone was walking across the floor of the room above.

According to the police officer, the footsteps moved diagonally across the room in a south-east to north-west direction. But the sound of footsteps was not all that was heard. It seemed as if something heavy was being dragged across the room and the rattling of what could have been a chain, but that particular noise was not easy to define. The footfalls moved forwards and backwards until at last the men plucked up courage to investigate the noises.

First of all they went to see if one of the dogs had found its way up the stairs, though it was unlikely that this was the cause of such a rumpus. On opening the kitchen door, the dog was seen to be lying quite contentedly on the floor. A thorough search revealed nothing. During the time the men were looking for the cause of the noise nothing else was heard.

For the next hour or so the conversation was confined to speculation about the mysterious and somewhat startling noises. At a quarter to eleven, when the guests were having supper, this time in the dining-room, the noises, exactly as before, were heard again. Again the men went upstairs – but as before nothing was found.

Most disturbing, you might say, but this is by no means the only strange event. There are people whose experiences have been even more startling, and perhaps more convincing.

Mrs Proctor, who helps as a guide taking parties round the Hall, actually saw the cowled head of a monk. It was during the summer of 1966. She was sitting on the settee in the lounge when she heard three knocks on the door leading into the room. She turned, thinking that perhaps it was Mrs Howarth returning with the tea she had been preparing, when, to her surprise, she saw a face peering at her through the window.

Mrs Proctor described it as best she could. 'It was a very pale face and it was not human. Over the head was what appeared to be a dark woollen cowl and the face was expressionless. As suddenly as it had appeared so it vanished.' Some time afterwards a pageant was held in the grounds of Chingle Hall depicting the house's history. Mrs Proctor looked at the figure of a monk which she thought was someone depicting the Blessed John Wall – but it was this same figure she had seen staring, devoid of expression at her some time before through the sitting-room window.

If unusual noises have been heard, pictures have rattled as if by their own volition and an unearthly figure has been seen, then whatever is at Chingle Hall also has the ability to move physical objects – including people.

Mrs Walmsley was standing in the lounge when suddenly someone gave her a violent push in the middle of her back which sent her sprawling across the room. Naturally, the first reaction would be to remonstrate with the person concerned, but on this occasion it wasn't so easy, in fact it proved impossible, because there was no one in the room with her – she was quite alone.

One guest who was unable to be present, Mrs Moorby, asked to speak to me on the telephone and told me of a weird experience she had at the Hall. She was upstairs in the bathroom, without any thoughts of the supernatural. In fact, Mrs Moorby is a sceptic, but what happened whilst she was in the bathroom gave her cause for some considerable alarm.

Once in the bathroom she developed a feeling that something wasn't quite right. It was as though she was being watched by something unseen. This feeling became stronger, and although she could not actually see anything, she began to feel terrified. The room became horribly cold, and she couldn't move. With a considerable amount of effort she managed to open the bathroom door and run down the stairs, and she distinctly remembers that she heard the bathroom door slam shut behind her.

Mrs Robinson, a friend of Mrs Howarth, had been invited to the Hall together with other guests. They had heard about the strange noises, but, like others, they were sceptical; in fact the whole business was treated as a joke, until certain events took place! First of all Mrs Robinson heard footsteps ascending the stairs. She, together with her husband, climbed the stairs and went into the room where the priest's hiding hole had been discovered. One of them knocked on the wall just above the aperture and to their amazement three knocks were heard coming from *inside* the priest's hole!

A series of happenings followed. Again footsteps were heard ascending the stairs, not just once more, but several times. There was a knock on the front door, but there was no one there when the door was opened. It was a night of startling occurrences to say the least.

Mrs McKay is quite convinced that there are two ghosts at Chingle Hall, and she may well be right. She was standing in the Priest's Room with a party of people when she felt patches of cold sweep over her. There were some honesty flowers in the room and they began to twist, as though someone was forcing them round. Eventually all the flowers actually shook, as did a table-lamp and a picture. The picture stopped moving as soon as Mrs McKay put her hand on it, and the flowers and the lamp stopped moving of their own accord.

Mrs Rigby, who was temporarily living in a caravan with her husband on the estate, had a strange experience. She was sitting with Mrs Howarth in the lounge, chatting over a cup of tea, when a plaque, an old wooden galleon, shot off the fireplace and dropped on the carpet in the centre of the room. There was no one else in the room but the two ladies, yet the plaque hurtled towards them as though thrown by an unseen hand.

Mrs Howarth's brother, William Strickland, has actually seen the figure of what appeared to be a priest walk through the gate and into the field but found nothing when he left the house to find out who the person was. On numerous occasions Miss Ann Strickland, Mrs Howarth's sister, has heard knocking, and the sound of footsteps and tappings.

I previously mentioned that one of the persons I met believed that there are in fact two ghosts, and the experiences of a man and his wife seem to give some support to this.

Mr and Mrs Jepson visited Chingle Hall as guests at a barbecue. During the festivities the late Mr Howarth asked them if they would care to look round the place. They were delighted to have the chance and as everyone else was outside they had the house to themselves, which gave them ample opportunity to view the Hall at their leisure. While they were downstairs in the room where the old oak cross was discovered, Mr Jepson was amazed to see two figures appear in front of him. They were dressed in monks' habits and they faced the cross as though they were praying. Gradually these two figures dissipated – they seemed to melt into the wall.

After this incident, which was not mentioned until some time afterwards by Mr Jepson, the couple went upstairs and entered the Priest's Room. When they had been there for a few minutes they left and went into the adjoining room which is the bedroom immediately above the porch. It was in this room that Mrs Jepson saw the figure of a man with pointed features and shoulder-length hair walk by the window. Mr Jepson turned round and said to the late Mr Howarth, 'This house is haunted, isn't it?' Mr Howarth smiled and admitted that it was.

Mrs Jepson then realised that the figure she had seen outside the window must have been very tall as the window is at least twelve feet above ground level! All three saw the 'apparition'. The interesting aspect about this is that neither Mrs Jepson nor her husband knew anything at all about the Hall and they were certainly not aware of it being haunted.

These accounts are well authenticated, but what about Mrs Howarth herself? She too has had a number of experiences. She says that the ghost has been heard on many occasions and several times tappings have been heard on the walls and furniture. Flowers have been shaken by some unseen hand.

Years ago, before they knew anything about the religious history of the house, Mrs Howarth and her husband moved into the room over the porch on the occasion when her mother came to visit her, and they experienced some very strange events. As soon as they were settled in bed the door latch lifted noisily and the door opened. This happened almost every night. One night in particular the door opened six times and Mrs Howarth had to get out of bed each time to close it, making sure that the catch was securely down. Again it opened, and this time she was shocked to see an illuminated form in a cloak by the wall near her side of the bed. She nudged her husband and they both watched it for almost a quarter of an hour, when it seemed to become dimmer and dimmer and gradually fade away. The strange thing about all this was that neither of them was afraid.

Before I relate the experience of Des McKenna and myself, one other story is well worth knowing. In 1945, when Italian prisoners-of-war were employed on the land throughout parts of Britain, one of them arrived at Chingle Hall to help on the farm. He was told that he could sleep in the bedroom above the porch as it was the only one available. He was completely ignorant of the ghost story and retired to bed a little before midnight. In the early hours of the next morning he was heard screaming and shouting frantically on the landing, 'Spirit in room – I no stay!' He didn't!

From these accounts, Chingle Hall must be one of the most haunted houses in the British Isles. I must confess that after hearing so many well authenticated accounts I wondered what sort of night we were going to have.

It was a quarter to midnight when we entered the room above the porch and one thing I noticed was the fact that the bedroom door was wide open – I had ensured that it was closed when together with Des McKenna and the Chief Superintendent I had made a point of firmly fixing the latch in position. Who had opened the door? To this day I don't know.

I had brought a thermometer with me to indicate any rapid drop in temperature, but nothing so dramatic took place. About one o'clock I heard a groaning, it could have been a door opening, it could also have been a hundred and one different things – we were somewhat edgy.

Ten minutes later we visited the Priest's Room. The atmosphere there was, to say the least, uncomfortable; there was a feeling of depression and utter sadness. We returned to the bedroom above the porch and discussed what our reactions might be if we saw anything, and neither of us knew just how we would react – a comforting thought.

At a quarter to three we made another excursion to the Priest's Room and this time the light in that room had been turned off! I switched on the light and returned to the bedroom. We had been there only a few seconds when we heard a crash, as if someone had thrown a heavy object to the floor. The noise could have come from the Priest's Room, but I am not sure of this.

Again we visited the Priest's Room, this time at seven fifteen, and once again the light had been switched off. The vigil was now over, but the events were certainly not! I asked Mrs Howarth and her sister if they had at any time switched off the light in the Priest's Room – both of them stated that they had not done so because they knew what we wanted to do and did not wish to interfere in any way. I asked my companion, Des McKenna, to put down in writing his experiences and impressions of the night. When I received his letter a few days afterwards and carefully examined it the contents fitted in exactly with the facts as I had recorded them.

He refers to all the guests hearing the footsteps while we were in the sitting-room. What follows is Des McKenna's account of our stay at Chingle Hall.

'Firstly let me say that throughout most of that night I felt quite calm, but in the back of my mind I was apprehensive as to how I would behave if anything came to us that was evil. I rather think that my resistance to such things would not be very great, and I don't know if I would have had the presence of mind to pray, cross myself or to give the simple command, "Go to Hell!"

'For a few minutes I was in the haunted room on my own while you were in the bathroom, and during that time I continually looked over my shoulder and kept an eye on every corner of the room, and although I neither saw nor heard anything at all I was very glad to see you back.

'I suppose the first odd thing that happened was when you and I and everybody who had been invited were in the drawing-room downstairs. Mrs Robinson was talking to me on my right and her husband was sitting on my left. She was saying that one night in the Hall everybody heard loud footsteps above as if someone were dragging something behind them. As she was telling me this both she and I heard footsteps crossing the ceiling immediately above us. They went from above the fireplace across towards the Dulcitone. Everybody went quiet and Mrs Howarth said, "We are all here in this room." If I remember rightly there were thirteen of us. Again the footsteps came, exactly the same, only louder, and I heard something rattling, like a vase on a metal tray will shake with each footstep, or a window frame. Quite a lot of us went upstairs but there was no one there. But I would like to say that these footsteps seemed so ordinary, just like a rather heavy-footed person bounding across the top rooms of the house, that I was not in the least disturbed, nor can I feel that they were supernatural, so placid was the atmosphere upstairs. But there you are – we were all in the drawing-room, and quite a few of us did hear those steps, and there wasn't anybody else in the house.

'You said, Peter, that the door to the haunted room was closed before we finally went to spend the night there. Well, I can't swear to that, but it definitely was open when we went up.

'The night's temperature dropped just after midnight from nearly 60°F to around 57°F and remained fairly constant at that from about 12.20 a.m. Apart from one or two small noises which could have been no more than the house settling to sleep and one quite audible sort of "bang", I heard nothing in the haunted room, although once or twice there were tiny sort of "snap" noises, and two of these could have been the putting out of the switch at the door of the Altar Room. And this I can say, and will say definitely, that on going into that room about 2.15 a.m. the light was out, although we both thought it had been left on. The impression I had of that room was one of a very gentle melancholy. A quietly sad room; a room in which nothing seemed to matter very much. A room in which the very air seemed to weep. It may have been the light which came from an electric lantern hung from the ceiling, and which seemed mainly a bluish hue which gave it an air of infinite and indeterminate sorrow, but it affected me quite strongly, and I felt that if we were to see anything it would be in this room more than the other, and in fact I suggested my staying there on my own. I felt that if I went into the Priest's Hide in the corner I might disturb whatever might show itself, but we decided against this and on leaving the room we checked that the light *was left on* before we went back to the room above the porch. Within this room we slept a little, and on going back again to the Altar Room, again we found that the light had been turned out. We were later to learn that no one had been in that part of the house throughout the night.

'But the most amazing thing happened in the morning. About 9.30 a.m. we were talking with Mrs Howarth and her sister when you, on seeing the dog, asked if you could take it into the haunted room. Mrs Howarth said, "No", that the dog had been trained not to go upstairs, and she suggested that we took one of the puppies which were about, I suppose, two months old. So Twiggy, as one of them was called, went upstairs with us. As soon as it came to the corridor that led to the haunted room it started skulking about and whimpering. We went into the room and called it but it would only come within a yard of the threshold of the door, where it remained cowering in terror. Eventually Mrs Howarth came upstairs and after repeatedly calling in enticement, carried the dog over the threshold where it cowered in the centre of the room. It was in an agony of fright, much in the same way as a dog would be if you were whipping and beating it. All this time none of us felt anything wrong about the room. We went into the Altar Room and carrying the dog in again it evinced the same symptoms of extreme terror. Once more we went back to the haunted room and this time, for a while it was quite happy, although when Mrs Howarth carried the dog over the threshold for the last time as we left the room, I noticed that it lost control of its functions and wet itself.

'And that is about it. I have wondered about the dog quite a lot since. In the old days coal miners used to carry a canary in a cage with them when they went into the mines and as soon as the canary stopped singing they would get out because the mine was filling with gas, to which a canary is more sensitive than a human being. And in the same way I feel that the dog was much more sensitive to anything supernatural than we were. As a dog can hear much higher noises than we can, perhaps it can see or feel things much more than we can.

'My own view, for what it is worth, is that an entity perhaps still lives in that haunted room, and probably doesn't want disturbing. It didn't show itself to us because we only spent one night there and it probably knew we were trying to see it. And the best way to discourage anyone from spying on it is just not to materialise. On the other hand if it thought that someone was going to stay there regularly, like Mrs Howarth and her husband, or those two schoolboys, people who got into bed and settled down for the night and left the light *out*, then it would show itself in order to remind them whose room it was. I wonder perhaps if its astral body in which or out of which it can live is something rather like an overcoat to us, that can be left by a door ready for use, and maybe the dog saw this and was disturbed, but on coming back this overcoat type of thing had been removed from by the door, and then perhaps through carelessness or a macabre joke replaced once the dog was in the room.

'Who knows, Peter, it is all conjecture. I have tried to present a clear picture of what happened that night, both factually and my own impressions of it. If there is anything I have left out, or anything that seems ambiguous, I hope you will let me know.

'Thank God we both came out of it safely.'

This is not the end, there is a sequel. Five days after I arrived home I received a letter from Mrs McKay who had been at Chingle Hall with her son, Andrew. I quote part of it below.

'I promised Mrs Howarth that I would write to you and tell you what happened when Andrew and I left the Hall last night.

'As we walked towards our car, which was parked outside the

barn facing the house, we looked at the window of the room in which there is the priest-hole. There was a white (or light grey) robed figure at the window. It was not very distinct so my son turned the light of the car on. Immediately the light in the room exploded into a brilliant glow and the figure appeared black as in a negative film. Finally the light died down and there only remained the soft glow of light from the landing.' (Actually the soft glow of light to which Mrs McKay refers was that of the light in the Priest's Room.)

Such then were our experiences at Chingle Hall. I believe, in fact I am quite convinced, that the place has a spirit, but the influence is not evil; it is quite innocuous. As Mrs Howarth says, 'If it is the spirit of the Blessed John Wall there is no need to be afraid, he was a man of God.'

One more letter I received from a grammar school boy, who, with a companion, spent a night at Chingle Hall and wrote the following account.

'My companion in this venture was Brian Hammersley and at the time we were both fourteen years old. We spent the night of 9–10th August 1968 in the "haunted chamber" above the porch. We picked this particular night, for it was the night of the full moon and August is supposed to be the month in which John Wall was executed.

'We arrived at the Hall at 7.30 p.m. and were shown around the house by Mr Knowles, a friend of Mrs Howarth. While standing in the Priest's Room we heard a distinct tapping sound coming either from the ceiling or hollow wall. This tapping continued for a few minutes at intervals.

'After examining the haunted chamber we secured the latch of the door before going downstairs. At approximately 9.30 p.m. Mrs Howarth went upstairs to put a lamp in the haunted chamber. On returning she commented that the door to the haunted room was open. We all examined the open door before returning to the living-room. I was the last to go downstairs and I made quite sure the latch was fitted into place. On going to bed at 10.35 p.m. Brian and I discovered the door wide open, although no one had left the living-room since we had examined the door at 9.30 p.m.

'We had been in bed for only a few minutes when once again we heard a tapping sound coming from either the wall or ceiling of the haunted chamber. When we compared the directions of the knocking we had heard earlier in the evening with this knocking we came to the conclusion that the source of the knocking must have come from somewhere near to the entrance of the hollow wall in the Priest's Room. This tapping sound continued for over two hours, although the time lapse between the tapping could often be as long as twenty minutes.

'Shortly after 2 a.m. the most significent event of the night occurred. I was lying awake when suddenly I heard a very loud thud directly above my heard. I was aware of something hovering over my head, but I could not bring myself to turn my eyes to the ceiling. Without exaggeration I can say that every bone in my body locked, but I did manage to nudge Brian with my elbow. He turned round and instead of looking at me he looked at a point above my head and said, "Don't move, there is something above your head." He later described it as a light about the size of a hand which disappeared into the wall or four-poster bed above my head. Unlike me, Brian, who was lying next to me, did not hear the distinctive thud. This light must have been above my head for at least fifteen seconds, during five of which Brian saw this light. Perhaps this could be explained by the fact that Brian belongs to the Church of England, whereas I am a Catholic and at that time I was wearing some rosary beads. Blessed John Wall, as you know, was also a Catholic.

'At approximately 3.20 a.m. Brian informed me that he could see half a head of a monk looking in at us through the window. I also looked and saw what appeared to be a monk's head, but now we are not so sure we did see a monk's head. The reason for this is that we were very "jumpy" after the incident above my head. The window was leaded, made of very old glass which tended to distort everything seen through it. There was a lot of condensation on the window through which the moonlight poured. The main feature of this face was the hair which was combed back and he may have been wearing a hood.

'At approximately 6.30 a.m. the latch on the door began to move and the door swung partly open. At first I thought it was Mrs Howarth coming to see if we were all right. When no one entered I stirred Brian who agreed the door had opened slightly. He then went back to sleep. Ten minutes later I woke Brian to show him the door was slowly moving again. At this point we heard what might have been footsteps going down the corridor. On getting out of bed I peered round the door and saw nothing. Mrs Howarth later told us she had not been near the room that morning. Incredible though it may sound, especially the last paragraph of this account, this is what happened the night we visited Chingle Hall.

Peter Kennedy.'

What follows are the accounts connected with Chingle Hall, one of which concerns an ancient piece of wood which was discovered in the Priest's hide. R.H.G. are the initials of a friend (Roy H. Gough) who has helped me in some of my researches. The piece of wood was the object of psychometry which was undertaken by a Mr James Dale, friend of Mr Gough.

'On 27th November 1970 I delivered to James Dale the large inscribed piece of wood found in the Priest's Hide at Chingle Hall. The inscriptions on it are a carved W and a carved device including two circles. The wood was tied up in a large translucent dark green plastic sack so that his initial impressions could be recorded without seeing the object. I gave him no information relating to the object or where it came from. R.H.G.'

'Psychometry on large plastic bag – tied at one end, 29th November, 1970

'The first thing I get is the feeling of a "crocodile" and of associated state of placidness and of lying in wait, quite contented, till the right type of creature comes near, quite unexpecting, then I can "sink my teeth" into it, and leave my marks and/or scars. Feel I am an old timer at this, as though I have caught many, and one or two wretched creatures have lived to regret it.

'Now all of a sudden I see a bright yellowy "live" upright cross; with it the words "The Sword of Damocles" and an intense feeling of going to put everything, and everyone, right – to the point of almost an obsession. Yes, feel here that somebody here has an obsession that they are going to make people, force people, to see "their truth" or the truth as they see it. Really I feel there is the overcompensating, in a religious way, to cover the real shortage within themselves. As I think more about it, I see two marks engraved or embedded on what I take to be a saddle, yet I only sense it is a saddle. It looks like W.S, but the thing which catches my attention is that fact that I feel that W is really made up of two V's (VV) with the S yet can't quite grasp the implication.

'Now feel I will open the bag to touch whatever the contents may be. Whew! – as I do I hear and see a church organ, it nearly deafens me. How funny, as I do take it out I see it's a heavy piece of wood but instantly see a W carved on it, plus now a larger set of markings that account for my reference to the distorted W, and instead of an S, two circles which could easily be mistaken as an S.

'As I concentrate on it I sense a powerful male person, with robes on, which I would link with a bishop, because he has a type of hat like this: Get grey hair, a strong pair of steel blue eyes and think of a person well built for his years, could have had a fine physique in his younger days, felt as I see him, he could have been about 80 years.

'As I place my hand on this block of wood, I keep getting very strong waves, a very powerful force and I keep getting a letter B; don't get the word, yet sense in length only, it is like Babylon.

'Now I go to 1943 when I felt there was a crashing (cracking?) or a neglected state that made me sad, causing me to feel irritable about something I was forced to recognise within myself, that I did not want to concede or acknowledge; feel I still dont' want to, if it comes to that. It is all part and parcel linked with this strong feeling. Don't feel it is because somebody wants to hurt anyone, more or less it's because, behind it all, they don't want to be hurt. Feel there is a very big, and I mean big, even large, disappointment behind it all. Feel I want to say it's all linked with Ronnie running away, as though this person (not Ronnie) is trying to prove to himself and to others that really they themselves are not responsible for it happening, that they would be incapable of causing it. If you asked them about it, they would deny they said anything, or did anything which caused it. I feel that I could say, doing nothing, steering clear, can cause things to happen by dodging responsibility just as much, if not more effectively, than if you actually did anything.

'This person who I'm talking about is trying to push things over to others, to try to force the "truth" down their throats so to speak, to cover over and hide their true shortage. What they are trying to push over to others "could or could not" be true and may well be believed by this person himself, but it is the inner motive of emptiness within and wanting others to "look up to them" that is behind it and this compensatory state. Rather than getting themselves corrected and letting the world sort itself out, including the WS.

J.D.'

Another friend, Barrie Colvin, together with Roy Gough and friends, visited Chingle Hall on 26th November 1970. The following is an account of their visit.

Visit to Chingle Hall by Barrie and Roy (26–11–70)

'*7.30 p.m.* Arrived at Chingle Hall with Roy and met Mrs Howarth, Miss Strickland, Mrs Eaves, Peter Moare and Dr James Dickie. We chatted by the fireside in the dining-room. Roy and I showed Peter and James around the Hall and they told us of their experiences at Cumberland.

'*10.10 p.m.* A noise was heard (metallic sound) by myself, Roy, Mrs Howarth, Miss Strickland and Mrs Eaves which appeared to come from the vicinity of the Chapel Room. Roy and I immediately investigated but saw nothing unusual in the Chapel Room. However, the outside door was open and had a metal ornament propped against it to prevent it from closing. A cat was also found in the porch and we noticed that the wind was quite strong outside – we therefore attached no significance to this noise (Peter and James were at this time upstairs, and Peter later stated that he had also heard this noise whilst sitting in the room above the porch (RAP). He said that it appeared to come from outside – by the bridge.

'Mrs Eaves told us of her recent encounter with the ghost. She was just entering the Hall through the outer door, when she saw a green diffuse figure approach her from the inside. It walked towards her and they met in the porch. She stopped suddenly and immediately the figure turned and walked back into the dining-room and closed the door behind it. This happened at 7 p.m. on the night of 25th November 1970.

'*12.15 a.m.* Peter and James left for Lancaster and as they did they investigated the possibility of car headlights causing a bright glare in the Priest's Room (PR) – ref. Mrs McKay and Andrew. They found that there was no possibility of this being the true cause of the bright light in the window.

'*12.30 a.m.* Went to bed in the RAP. Roy slept on the bed, I slept on the floor, close to the door, so that if it opened it would hit my head and wake me.

'*12.40 a.m.* I got up and placed the bar of the door latch in such a position that the door would open if given a push from the outside. I noticed, whilst lying on the floor, that there was quite a strong draught passing through the room. We therefore had optimum conditions in favour for an opening of the door.

'*8.50 a.m.* We got up after a very peaceful night and went down to breakfast.

'*9.15 a.m.* Mrs Howarth recalled the experience of Mrs Proctor. It was about 4 p.m. on 26th October, when Mrs Proctor walked into the Chapel Room and to her amazement noticed that a small plant in the window began to shake violently from side to side. Several other people saw this phenomenon (Mrs Proctor was showing some visitors around the Hall) and all of them were quite amazed. There were apparently no signs of a breeze in the room, in fact the air was very still outside.

'The most striking account of psychic phenomena came from Mrs Howarth whilst we were eating breakfast. The night after our last visit to Chingle Hall, Mrs Howarth had some unexpected guests and decided to sleep in the guests' room (first on the right at the top of the stairs). She went to bed at 11.45 p.m. but due to the fact that the bulb had gone in the room, she had to leave the door open in order to get some light from the hallway. She got into bed, and after lying there for about 5 minutes, the light suddenly went on. She noticed that it glowed very brightly indeed, much brighter than the usual low-wattage bulb in that room. The light stayed on for about a minute and then went off. Mrs Howarth then tried to turn the light back on by using the switch by her bed and also by getting up and using the wall switch. The light remained off.

'The next night this phenomenon occurred three times, so Mrs Howarth called her electrician. He examined the bulb in the guests' room and made it clear that the bulb was broken and could not possibly give any light.

'*10.15 a.m.* Borrowed the piece of wood from the priest's hole in the PR and left Chingle Hall.

B. G. Colvin, 30–11–70'

Unusual happenings take place at Chingle Hall. It has the reputation of being one of the most haunted houses in the country. I feel that there is a need for much more investigation, and who knows what will be discovered in the future?

Liverpool

To be Forewarned

Many people have been prevented from encountering disaster by a voice, quite audible, but belonging to no one, for no other person has been present. I remember the story, though not the source, of a private soldier who, while serving in India, was walking along a mountain road where to his right were precipitous heights of rock and scrub and to his left a sheer drop of hundreds of feet. He approached a bend in the track and quite clearly heard a voice say, 'Stop, there is danger.' He instantly halted and waited for a few minutes. Suddenly there was a tremendous crash. Splintered boulders were hurled scores of feet into the air, and tons of rock swept over the track and down into the valley below.

Had the soldier not instantly obeyed the voice he would certainly have been crushed to death in that avalanche of rock. He looked round to see if there was anyone present who had foreseen the danger before he could have done, but there was no one. The soldier claimed that he did not hear the sound of falling rock until at least a minute or more after the voice had told him to stop, and he firmly believed that it was the work of some supernatural force.

Some thing of a similar kind happened to a very well-known film and theatre actor who wrote to me at length giving me details of his adventure. I shall refer to him as Mr X. He is a friend of the vicar of Shifnal in Shropshire and when the vicar moved into the vicarage he invited Mr X to visit him. It was Mr X who, as he first set foot in the vicarage, a place he had not visited previously and who knew nothing of its reputation as a haunted house, said that he was certain that there was a presence in the place.

He told me that he has had a number of unusual experiences but normally dismisses them as quickly as possible, although there were two incidents that have left indelible marks on his mind for which he could offer no explanation.

He was taking the leading part in a ballet which he had also produced. The company were to play at Liverpool when he was taken seriously ill and the doctor strictly forbade him to travel from London for the opening night. There was no one to take his place and he knew that unless he could be there the performance would end in disaster. He foolishly defied his doctor's orders, left his sick bed and somehow got to Liverpool. The journey was a nightmare, for the effects of his illness were beginning to tell on him. He virtually staggered into the theatre and managed to make-up and get himself on to the stage.

Two-thirds of the way through the performance, when his part in the ballet demanded that he carry a heavy cross on the way to his grave, he felt all physical strength being drained from him. He fell to the floor and was unable to move. Mentally he cried, 'Jesus, help me.' It was a phrase that came into his mind because of the extremity of his condition. Quite suddenly something very strange and quite inexplicable happened. He felt himself physically lifted up as if by strong hands and from that moment onwards he was no longer ill. Not only did he recover for the performance, but the serious illness left him completely.

In his letter he writes, 'I am not a very good person and did not deserve the miraculous thing to happen to me.'

Let us look at this experience more closely. We can be absolutely certain that Mr X was seriously ill; the doctor's strict orders to stay in bed, especially in view of the importance of the production, is evidence of the grave concern for his patient. He knew that to travel to Liverpool and then take his part in the ballet would be little short of suicide.

Mr X was also aware of the seriousness of his condition but as a dedicated actor he believed that 'the show must go on' although he was under no misapprehension about what the consequences might be. I believe that at one point in the performance he feared that he was dying, and in desperation he called on the name of Jesus. That the cure was permanent is proof that it was not will-power alone that enabled him to carry on.

He told me of another unusual experience that happened when he was alone on the stage of a Nottingham theatre. During the performance he heard a voice distinctly say, 'Stand back.' At first he took no notice and went on with his part. Again the voice said, 'Stand back.' After a third time he did as the voice commanded and within seconds of his retreat a large arc light came crashing to the stage and landed exactly where he had been standing.

He says that the voice he heard was not a human one but an inner voice, compelling and forceful. This he attributes to the supernatural ability of some benevolent spirit which had the power to communicate with him.

These are strange stories, but they are true. I am convinced we are not alone, but in some mysterious way are in contact with another world, call it the spirit world, the astral plane, or give it whatever name you wish.

The Phantom Nun

Spectres of monks and nuns long dead seem to be some of the commonest kinds of wraiths. There must be many houses or flats built on what were once monastery or convent sites. Less than half a mile from where I live there is a fine Georgian building, now a public house, reputed to be haunted by the ghost of a monk, and researches have revealed that the house was built on land where once a monastery stood many centuries ago.

The house has been the 'local' for a comparatively short time. Previously it was a private house, but it remained empty for many years and had an uncanny reputation. There were few who would walk past it in the dark. More than one person has testified to having seen and heard something ghostly, and some say that they have identified the form of a monk, with head and face hidden by a huge cowl, walking through the house.

The monk is seen no more, or so it seems, for no one has mentioned him since the house became what it is today. I don't know if an exorcism took place or if it left of its own accord, but there are now no disturbances that could be attributed to the supernatural.

I have heard many accounts of hauntings by monks and nuns and in most they have evoked no fear but have added a kind of warmth and comfort to the places where they have appeared. After all, they were men and women of God who had, in their earthly days, devoted themselves to acts of charity.

About fifteen years ago in Wandsworth, London, there was a case of haunting which took place in a block of flats, and one of the tenants was so disturbed by events that she appealed to the local council for help. The flats had been converted from a convent into a huge and rambling block. It was a maze of corridors and dark places, housing over thirty families, and quite a number of them have had frightening and disturbing experiences.

One tenant, Mrs S, who had lived there for over eight years, claimed that she had several times seen the ghost of a nun, dressed in black. Mrs S lived in a spacious first-floor flat which was believed to have been the mother superior's room. Her experiences began almost as soon as she and her family had moved in. On the first occasion they were all sitting in one of the rooms, when a gust of wind blew right through the flat – although all the doors and the windows were closed.

A few weeks later her sister-in-law, Mrs C, came to live with her and on one occasion she was washing up in the kitchen and apparently holding a conversation with Mrs S, but Mrs S was elsewhere in the flat. Now Mrs S had overheard Mrs C, and afterwards asked to whom she was speaking. She replied, 'Why, I was speaking to you; you were standing right behind me', but Mrs S had not been in the kitchen.

There was always a feeling that they were being watched by some unseen presence, but this presence was not to remain invisible for long. Both women have several times seen a dark spectre. It had no definite shape, no hands, no face, no voice – just a dark rustling shape. According to Mrs S, the apparition begins its walk near the big fireplace in the living-room and glides through the hall and then disappears in the entrance to the bathroom. She followed her along what she named the 'nun's walk'. Neither Mr S nor Mr C would believe their wives; they merely laughed and said that it was only an association of ideas with the place, and what it had been in past years. They were both extremely sceptical until something happened which terrified Mr C. He came into the living-room, his face as white as a sheet and trembling violently. When he was asked the reason for his condition he said in a shaking voice, 'I've just seen your lady.'

There is another part of the building where it is possible the old convent chapel once stood. It was on the landing that Mrs M saw and heard the phantom. She was asleep and was awakened by a sense that something was wrong. It was a feeling which she could describe only as an overwhelming sense of something or someone near to her. She switched on the light, but there was no one in the bedroom. Hurriedly putting on a dressing-gown, she ran on to the landing to go to the children's bedroom to see if all was as it should be there. She had no sooner opened her bedroom door when she froze in her tracks – standing right in front of her by a table which she kept on the landing was the dark figure of a nun. Mrs M says that she saw the face of the spectre. There was nothing evil about it; in fact she remembers that it was a pleasant, roundish face. She heard the nun speak, as if addressing Mrs M. 'Don't be afraid, just say, God be with you.' After this the apparition was engulfed in the gloom of the landing and in a short time had disappeared. Mrs M could not move for some considerable time as she was so terrified.

Mrs M owned a sideboard, a very modern piece of furniture and quite out of keeping with the room. It was from this sideboard that there had come strange and rather ominous tappings. One evening a friend was visiting Mrs M and the tappings began – they were definitely coming from the inside of one of the cupboards. When the cupboard door was opened a gust of wind blew into the room and both women were certain that the gust came from within the sideboard.

On another occasion Mrs M had staying with her a guest who saw the casement windows open as if by some unseen hand. But this was followed by something even more frightening – the bedclothes were violently thrown off the bed and piled in a heap on the floor. On another evening her children rushed into the living-room crying, and had obviously been badly frightened. When she asked them what was the matter, they said they had seen the 'nurse' again – she had been looking at them through a window. Being young, the children had mistaken the habit of the nun for the uniform of a nurse.

There was also a family living in what was called the chapel wing, who said they often heard the soft tread of numerous feet crossing their ceiling, like a procession of nuns going to prayer, but no one lives upstairs in that part of the block because there is no flat above.

Such then have been the unnerving experiences of some families in that converted convent. Yet it seems that the spectre of the nun is not in any way meant to frighten people, but she has been given the title the 'sinister sister' perhaps somewhat unjustly, although one can appreciate the alarm it must cause the residents from time to time. After all, it's not everyone who can expect to meet the dead when they go from one room to another.

Shropshire

A Ghostly Cortège

Have you ever spent a cold winter's night stranded in a car on some lonely road with only the falling snow for company? If you have been so unfortunate as to experience such a plight, then you will fully appreciate the fear that begins to gnaw at the mind. As the temperture drops and your toes and fingers become numb with the cold, so one's fear of entombment is heightened.

The severity of winter has sometimes claimed its victims who have been caught in some lonely high place on the fells. The roads, because of thickly falling snow, have brought cars to a halt and the thought of a night without food and warmth among such stark desolation brings no comfort of mind, only the prospect of physical discomfort and, who knows, perhaps a snow-bound grave.

To sleep in such circumstances is fatal, for it could result in the sleep of death, painless perhaps, but almost certain. My story is about such a happening, but to add to this dreadful turn of events there was already, inside the vehicle, a corpse.

The story takes us back nearly forty years when an undertaker was asked to convey the body of a dead monk to a monastery some eighty miles distant. At this time the undertaker was a young man who proudly possessed a recent acquisition to the business, a shining new hearse. He had often been asked if he was afraid of the dead, to which he replied, 'It's not the dead we ought to fear, but the living.' During his young days he claimed he was an atheist, quite cynical about the existence of God, but his views were changed by a strange experience which, on reflection, he believed to be an answer to prayer, a prayer which was uttered in panic and fear.

It was about four o'clock in the afternoon when he was urgently requested to convey a coffin containing the body of a monk to a distant monastery. It seemed a long journey to make at such short notice, but evidently the coffin had to be taken and there was a real sense of urgency.

It was almost dark when he set out in falling snow for the monastery. The hearse, although new, had not been out recently and this was to be its first journey of any distance. The undertaker began in high spirits but his enthusiasm seemed to gain the upper hand and instead of keeping to the main road, a route which he knew reasonably well, he decided to attempt a short cut by way of narrow country lanes, but this was his undoing. The result of this foolhardy venture was a complete loss of direction, and no amount of searching could produce familiar landmarks by which he could reorientate himself.

Then it happened. The hearse came to a halt in a deep snowdrift and was almost buried. In vain he tried to start up the car, but without success. He took hold of the starting handle and attempted to get out of the vehicle, but the snow had blocked the doors. He was buried alive in this unusual tomb, and he was not alone. There was little comfort in knowing that he was sharing this experience with a 'corpse'. A thought struck him: here they were, the two of them – the dead and the living dead.

Outside the hearse the bitter wind howled, the swirling snow obliterating everything, then suddenly, as if by command, the wind dropped and there was an eerie stillness. In desperation he tried to open the door but it was still firmly held. Through the window he could see millions of stars looking down on a white shrouded world. The snow, no longer whipped along by the wind, lay motionless. Reality, however, soon stabbed him awake to his fearful plight. Again and again he tried to open the door, but no amount of effort could move it.

He sat there in utter despair. The temperature had dropped considerably and there came the realisation that it was freezing. Gradually he would freeze to death. Soon he would be like the corpse in the coffin. His thoughts turned to his wife. Strange that an undertaker should meet his end like this, and he burst into hysterical laughter. The situation was quite ludicrous, but it was real. He became terrified. What was death really like? He who had witnessed so much death was about to die in an icy tomb.

He began to pray, and he prayed as few men have ever done, sometimes shouting, sometimes silently, but they were desperate prayers. At last he became more controlled, thinking of nothing in particular. Eventually he became aware of some unseen presence. Perhaps it was the utter loneliness of the place that was playing tricks with his mind, but he felt warmer. A glow crept through his body and the snow and ice on the windows began to melt. He peered out at the white stillness.

Twelve hooded figures in black were approaching the hearse and as they passed close by he distinctly heard the chanting. Outside it was still freezing, but his body was all aglow. Had his prayers been answered? Who or what were the figures? The cortège continued for about a hundred yards beyond the hearse and then they turned around and returned. As they passed a second time the snow seemed to be brightly illuminated and there was music in the air, music of a kind that was unearthly, a sweet music that brought a feeling of happiness and a sense that all would be well – now there was no fear of death.

The night became peaceful and he fell asleep. He was awakened by someone tugging at the car door. Some workmen were trying to open it and he could hear people walking about on the frozen snow. When the workmen finally opened the door they were amazed to find him alive. They said that his survival was nothing less than miraculous. Welcome hands helped him out of the hearse and a drink of coffee from one of the workmen's flasks soon revived him. The car was dug out, and eventually the undertaker was able to resume his journey.

He related the events to the abbot, who agreed that his prayers must have been answered. But who were the ghostly hooded figures? They were certainly not portents of death. Had they come in answer to his prayer? Was it the distraught mind of a man under a tremendous strain? We shall never know.

Shropshire

Evil at the Inn

Many inns of England are reputed to be haunted; just how many of them actually are is open to conjecture. It must be remembered that a number of our hostelries go a long way back in history and were the focal point in community life, especially that of a village. It is not surprising therefore that tales of haunted beer cellars, footsteps along dimly lit passages, faces at windows, have been handed down from one generation to another.

Country inns of course are more suited to such tales and many of these places have a room or rooms in which the wraith of a former occupant, be it landlord or guest, is supposed to visit. The country pub, set back from the lonely road, deep in the heart of some bleak moorland spot, with its wooden sign swinging in the wind and its rusty hinges issuing ghostly creaks, creates just the right atmosphere for a haunting, whether it be fact or fiction.

A short time ago I visited one such place and spoke to the landlady, a widow who had been there eight years. When I mentioned that I had heard that it was haunted, she laughed and in a broad Staffordshire accent replied, 'Well then, tha's cum to a place 'ere, if there's a ghost 'ere then I an a (have not) seen it.'

The place looked ripe for a haunting, but I was out of luck – if the landlady said there was no ghost, then she ought to know! So I drank my half of bitter and wished her goodbye. I couldn't help noticing a smile on her face. Perhaps she thought that it was a little odd for a complete stranger to be talking about such things. When outside I looked at the inn. It didn't seem right that it should not have a ghost. Still, that's the way it goes; not every place reputed to have a ghost can boast of a real one!

The following story happened over fifty years ago to a person known to me and who is well versed in Shropshire folklore, legends and hauntings. He is a true Salopian, having lived all his life in that county. It seems that he possesses acute psychic qualities, for he has had a number of experiences which he claims are nothing less than a glimpse of the supernatural.

As a youngster he and his mother, who had only recently been widowed, were invited to spend Christmas with the landlord of an inn situated on the border of Shropshire. The place was by a lonely road and there was a magnificent view of the Welsh hills.

The proprietor of the inn had been a friend of the family and felt sorry for the bereaved woman, so he invited her and the boy to spend the festive season with him. The villagers thought him an odd character, an eccentric, and yet he was a kindly person, as could be seen in his concern for the widow.

They were given a warm welcome and a hot meal. That evening they went to bed early. The young boy slept in the same room as his mother and he distinctly remembers bolting the door before making preparations for bed.

He had been asleep for some time when he was awakened by someone knocking at the door. He jumped out of bed and in a tremulous voice asked who was outside. There was no answer, so he slipped back the bolt and attempted to open the door, but it could not be moved. He was about to call out again when suddenly the door blew open and a gust of wind blew violently into the room. His first reaction was to go to the window, but when he opened it he saw that the night was calm and peaceful. After bolting the door again he climbed back into bed and was soon asleep. Some time after, he was aroused again by the same knocking and once more he tried to open the door but it was firmly closed.

Panic gripped the lad and he called loudly for his mother, who had, up to this time, been sleeping undisturbed. She tried to comfort him by telling him that he had had a nightmare, but he was not convinced and called out loudly for the landlord. He was fast asleep, oblivious to what was going on.

After another five minutes or so he tried the door again and this time it opened. Once again they were asleep, but not for long. He was awakened by a cold hand passing over his face. He screamed, but his mother slept on. A little later footsteps were heard. Someone was coming up the stairs. Slowly the steps came to the landing and moved along the corridor and halted at the bedroom door. He shouted, 'Who's there?' There was no answer. The door slowly opened.

A sinister influence was moving about the bedroom but there was nothing to be seen. Attempts to sleep failed and only fitful dozing followed. Suddenly there was a scratching on the window. Again he screamed and this time his mother got out of bed. He was convinced that there was someone in the room. The mother tried to soothe her son, but it was obvious he was terrified. She was just about to lie down when the bedclothes were flung on the floor by some unseen hand. They were replaced, but were again thrown with considerable force to the floor. This happened three or four times.

Each time they tried to sleep, a strange tapping came from under the bed, and this was followed by footsteps, as though someone was walking round the room searching for something. Then the boy saw something that paralysed his vocal chords. He was in a state of utter terror. There, at the foot of the bed, was an old lady with a horribly wizened face. She beckoned the boy and his mother to follow her.

They followed her downstairs, through the kitchen and into the cellar. The figure stopped, pointed to a slab of stone and then gave a high-pitched and unearthly scream and vanished, while they stood paralysed with fear. Somehow they managed to get back to their bedroom, but sleep was impossible.

The next morning they told the landlord of their experience. 'I don't know how to get shut of it, that's why nobody stops here,' was all he could say.

The same day a clergyman was called in and after relating their story he agreed to come back that night and exorcise the spirit. In the meantime they persuaded the landlord to raise the slab of stone in the cellar. The remains of a skeleton were discovered. The clergyman, true to his word, arrived that night and after a prayer of exorcism left the inn. From that time onwards the spirit did not trouble the place again.

Later they learned that about a hundred and fifty years ago an old lady had come to stay at the inn with her daughter. The latter was murdered by a stranger during the night and the body buried in the cellar.

Madam Piggott - The Chetwynd Ghost

One and a half miles north of Newport in Shropshire, on the A41, is the village of Chetwynd. South-west of Chetwynd is the larger village of Edgmond, the distance between them being about two miles as the crow flies, but slightly more by road. The villages figure prominently in the story of the hauntings by the ghost of Madam Piggott.

At one time this apparition was quite troublesome in the area, many people had seen her and some had been terrified. Fear of the ghost became so intense that numerous clergy were called upon to exorcise this earthbound 'spirit' – but without success. Twelve local clergymen attempted to lay the ghost by reading psalms by the Windy Oaks, a favourite place for Madam Piggott's appearances, but even this was unsuccessful. The numerous appearances of Madam Piggott and the time when she was most troublesome are well authenticated.

She walks the lanes and fields of that area to this day. A few years ago it was reported in the national press that a motorist saw a figure in white cross in front of his car. He was certain that he had knocked someone down. When he got out of the car he expected to find a body, but to his amazement no one was there. This experience considerably upset him and he reported it to the police; they found nothing. What the driver saw was probably the ghost of Madam Piggott. By the roadside where the incident took place is the churchyard; could it be that she was returning to her grave, to rise again and wander about the countryside?

The area has been haunted by the ghost of Madam Pigggott for over two hundred years. She was the wife of the Squire of Chetwynd Hall and was expecting her first baby; naturally the Squire hoped for a son who would inherit the estate. But there were complications before the birth, as the Squire's wife contracted smallpox. The doctor found himself in a dilemma and told the Squire that he feared the loss of the unborn child or the mother. The Squire replied, 'Lop the root to save the branch.' His wife heard the death sentences pronounced by her husband and one can imagine the anguish she must have felt.

Unfortunately, neither mother nor child lived, and the distraught woman apparently could find no rest for her soul. Her ghost was seen to emerge on several occasions from a trap door in the roof of Chetwynd Rectory, which was demolished in 1864, though why from the Rectory and not the Manor is still a mystery.

Her ghost also frequented the stump of an old oak tree in the area known as the Windy Oaks, and the stump became known as 'Madam Piggott's armchair'. There she sat weeping and combing the baby's hair. When anyone rode past on horseback, it is said that she climbed up behind them until they came to a stream beyond which they were unable to go. This so alarmed the people that many attempts were made by 'bell, book and candle' to exorcise the spirit. Modern roads carrying an ever increasing number of vehicles have not in the least frightened the ghost away.

Three men, one of whom was the late Elliott O'Donnell, decided about forty years ago to investigate. The two other men were Mr Byford-Jones and a Mr Talbot who had met the ghost some time before. Many people, including Mr Talbot, had been terror stricken by its awful appearance. Men and women had been badly scared, for the apparition had the unpleasant habit of following them along the Windy Oaks, the lonely stretch of tree-sheltered road. It was not only the appearance of Madam Piggott which was frightening, but also a terrible and unearthly noise like a deep-throated growl. Mr Talbot had been riding home on his motorcycle when the ghost confronted him, and when he accelerated to get away he still had the sensation of being followed.

The ghost-hunting trio walked through the long avenue of trees which was about a mile long. Not a sound could be heard except footsteps of the three men. The moon shone eerily through the twisted branches of the gnarled oaks, the path was almost ankle-deep in dead and rotting leaves, and the branches of the trees almost met over the road.

The investigators reached a part of the Windy Oaks where Chetwynd Church spire could be seen through the trees, and here they halted. O'Donnell left Byford-Jones and Talbot together, walked forty yards ahead and stopped. Suddenly Talbot gripped Byford-Jones's arm and pointed to a vibrating light among the trees. Shortly afterwards they heard a long, low, unearthly, but animal-like growl.

O'Donnell returned and said that he too had seen a tall column of white light from where he had stood. All three saw this column of light making erratic movements first in one place, and then in another. Again they heard the noise, which was now more like a snarl.

There was a pool not far away and from it there suddenly came a tremendous din. Wildfowl and moorhens screamed and birds in the trees made fantastic noises. The men had remained silent and still, so the wild disturbance could not have been caused by any movement of theirs.

O'Donnell, while on his own, had the impression that he was being followed, but he saw no one; then he heard the strange, low, ominous growl which was often repeated. The light which he saw among the trees was cylindrical in shape and about six feet high. He had the impression that it was a female form enveloped in a shroud. No features or limbs were visible, only a vague outline, and when the light vanished the sounds continued for a while.

When the three men related their experiences at a local inn no one laughed, as many of the people there had had similar experiences.

Shropshire

The Figure in the Graveyard

Graveyards have always evoked a fear from people, indeed it takes a brave person to walk between the tombstones at dead of night. During the daytime it is of little consequence, but at night – well, that is a different matter. The place of the dead takes on a different and, one could say, a disturbing aspect.

I have been in many graveyards during the day and there has been a feeling of peace, sometimes I have been indifferent to any particular sense, but I have stood in a graveyard at night and felt quite nervous. As one walks among the headstones there is the constant feeling of being watched, or even followed. It can be put down to imagination, but I wonder how many cynics would have the courage to walk through a remote graveyard at dead of night. The proof of their cynicism and scepticism might well be confirmed, on the other hand they may funk the attempt.

The story I have to tell concern two investigations of a reputedly haunted churchyard by the now ruined church at Broseley in Shropshire.

My first account takes us back forty years when Elliott O'Donnell, together with Mr Byford-Jones of the *Express and Star*, and a well-known Shropshire sceptic, Mr G. Davies, visited the churchyard. Elliott O'Donnell spent many night vigils in castles, houses, graveyards and country lanes, but he admitted that not one of them was as eerie as the graveyard by the ruins of the Red Church.

Today the once familiar landmark is no more. The tower and the ruins have been demolished, only the graveyard remains. The old church survived for over two hundred years. During its last years it stood neglected in a corner of a field where victims of a cholera plague are buried.

When our three intrepid ghost hunters went on their journey the church and its tower were still standing, but the building was only a shell. The interior was full of fallen masonry and debris and few windows remained unbroken. The founder of this particular church was Frances Turner Blithe of Brotch Hall, and the building was completed in 1770. Occasionally the founder was called Mary Brown, but no one seems to know why.

There have been many stories of ghostly visitations connected with the Red Church. It is said that the builders endeavoured to erect it at the bottom of the hill, but somehow the foundations were mysteriously removed to the top of the hill. There it remained, built in the position stated in the founder's will.

Mr Davies had been scoffing at the idea of anything supernatural being connected with the place, making out that it was a natural reaction of those who were frightened because their imaginations were allowed to rule their minds. However, on approaching the graveyard, Mr Davies began to show signs of uneasiness. He talked less frequently and gave the impression that he didn't like the place. There was, he confessed, an unusual and unpleasant atmosphere.

At about ten o'clock Davies said that he could see a figure in one part of the graveyard. O'Donnell said that he thought it to be the figure of a woman. Mr Byford-Jones gave a gasp and pointed to the corner of the graveyard where he too saw the figure of a woman. It was tall and dark and appeared to be wearing a poke bonnet and was carrying something in her hand, which could have been a candlestick. Davies' description of the figure was exactly the same as that of O'Donnell. The three men had been standing about twenty yards from the figure and they decided to follow her, but when they entered the graveyard there was no one to be seen. A thorough search revealed nothing – the figure had gone, but where? She made no noise as she glided on her way. There is little doubt that all three men saw the figure, and they are men whose evidence can be fully trusted.

A much more recent encounter with the strange figure comes from a man who was in that part of the country one Christmas Eve not long ago, when he decided to take a short cut by way of the graveyard. Suddenly he was startled by a bright moving light. He stood motionless and watched. There was a figure walking across the graveyard and it appeared to be carrying some form of light, probably a lantern. It was wearing a long, dark cloak and in the dark seemed to stand out almost as if its edges were luminous.

The figure was in fact coming towards him and he could distinctly see the face which was that of a beautiful young woman. He stood there, fascinated by the figure, unable to speak or move. Suddenly his blood began to tingle. He stretched out his hand to touch her, but it pushed through her. There was a sense of warmth and a feeling of what can only be described as gentleness. She passed by in the direction of the church. The windows of the church became illuminated and singing could be heard from within. A bell tolled three times, yet no bell remained in the old battered tower.

Some time afterwards, a photographer taking a picture of the ruins, left his camera by one of the gravestones while he walked round what remained of the church and when he returned he discovered his camera had been moved some distance from the place where he had left it, and there was no one else to be seen. The photographer was also puzzled by a picture he took of the church. A white figure could be seen on the photograph at one of the windows – yet there was no defect on the negative.

Who was the mysterious visitor to the burial ground? The answer will never be known. Was it the same wraith that was seen by the three men years earlier?

Elliott O'Donnell is quite correct in his assessment of the graveyard; it is an eerie place, even in broad daylight. The spectre still walks and yet she does not evoke fear. It could be that she was a person of very gentle disposition, kindly in her life, perhaps Frances Turner Blithe herself, who knows!

Shropshire

The Pool of Death

Woods, country lanes, fields and gardens sometimes reveal supernatural manifestations and some most sinister apparitions have been seen on stretches of water, especially lakes and ponds.

An acquaintance of mine, well known for his wide knowledge of folklore and legend, tells of a very unusual and mysterious event. In his early years he believed that there was a scientific explanation for every supernatural occurrence. But today he is of a different mind, for he has since encountered apparitions himself, some fearful to look at, others quite innocuous.

One particular apparition was that of a very beautiful lady, but a very dangerous one.

Near a sharp bend on one of the main roads in Shropshire was a deep pool, surrounded by bushes and trees, a sinister place even in full daylight. He was cycling home one night when it was very dark and all was as silent as the grave. As he approached the bend in the road a strange feeling came over him, as if someone or something was waiting for him. It was as if he were fulfilling a prearranged meeting. As he passed the pool he saw something like a white vapour hovering over its glossy surface. The reflection of the moon on the water added to the ghostly atmosphere.

The mist began to take shape and moved towards him. Rooted to the spot, he was unable to pedal his cycle any farther. The 'thing' seemed to draw him towards it. It had no definite outline, but it could have been the form of a woman enveloped in long white flowing garments. It passed right through the front wheel of his bicycle and a coldness brushed his face. Then it was gone, and he pedalled home faster than he had ever done before, not a little unnerved by his experience.

Next morning he told a friend about the previous night's encounter with this strange thing and to his surprise he learned that the pool was haunted, but by whom or what no one knew.

There followed a spate of accidents on that bend, some of them fatal, but whether they can be attributed to the 'spirit' is a matter for conjecture. Some motorists claimed that they had seen the luminous vision of what could have been a woman standing in the middle of the road. When cars approached, the figure hovered in front of them and hypnotised the drivers. Quite a number of accidents were reported in the national press and some credence given to supernatural intervention.

Was there some sinister influence connected with the pool, and if so what was it? The mystery had to be solved; so the cyclist who had first encountered the apparition, together with some friends and the local vicar, visited the pool one night to keep vigil and see if the apparition would once again show itself.

The night was dark and still, the moonbeams shone fitfully through scurrying clouds. The church clock struck twelve – and then it happened. Something was coming out of the pool. Slowly, and without rippling the surface of the water, there arose what appeared to be a long, slender white arm. It contrasted sharply with the ink-black surface of the water; it was luminous and radiated an uncanny light all around. Noiselessly the arm moved upwards and the watchers could then trace the form of a woman. For a few seconds it hovered over the centre of the pool and a strange perfume filled the air, and the form seemed to be casting a spell over the watchers as they walked towards the water.

How long this lasted it was difficult for them to say; all sense of time seemed to have vanished and they felt as if they were in a timeless vacuum, unable to control their movements. The figure was drawing them closer to the cold, uninviting and sinister water.

Somehow the vicar managed to utter a prayer, inarticulate and hardly audible, but it was sufficient to break the spell. Quickly he offered a prayer of exorcism and the spirit vanished. It has not been seen since, and there have not been any more accidents at that notoriously fatal spot.

On this last occasion the face of the apparition was plainly seen, and was that of a beautiful woman, whose features slowly changed until they expressed the utmost evil and terrible malevolence.

The only explanation for this manifestation is that the 'spirit' was intent on luring others to their deaths. Had she herself been the victim of a vile crime and her body thrown into the pool, or could she have been the perpetrator of a foul murder? Whatever the reason, she was bound by some tragedy to haunt that pool, her spirit unable to find rest until the vicar's prayer of exorcism put an end to the spirit's activities.

Exorcism is not always effective. I know of two exorcisms, one conducted by a bishop, neither of which was of any avail. It may be that some earthbound 'spirits' may not want to leave the places they haunt.

Now the pool no longer contains the evil influence and motorists can pass without fear of spiritual molestation. The water is still there, dark and forbidding, but the spell is broken and it no longer claims its victims. The malevolent wraith has gone.

The Spectre of a Beautiful Lady

It is often thought that all ghosts are to be feared, but I know of people who have been convinced that they have been in touch with the supernatural and have felt only a feeling of sorrow and compassion.

The man who told me the following story said that as a boy he had often heard of the Grey Lady of Badger Hall. He would listen for hours to the tales, little knowing that in time to come he himself would meet her more than once.

Those who have spent much time in ghost hunting have found that there are certain times of the year when the dead are more likely to be encountered than at any other time. Elliott O'Donnell believed that September and October are the most conducive to such manifestations. Most of his investigations were undertaken at this time of the year. Hallowe'en, October 31st, is regarded as the night when apparitions are most likely to be seen, the night when they rise from their graves. Christmas Eve, again according to O'Donnell, the dead are said to appear and he has spent a few such nights in solitary vigil; he was not usually disappointed.

Our story begins on one Christmas Eve many years ago when my informant was sitting by the fire almost asleep. He was brought back to full consciousness by a sudden noise, as if something was rustling near at hand. He looked up, and there standing by the far wall was a beautiful lady. Every feature was clearly defined. She was wearing a kind of grey silk dress and had light golden hair and was looking directly at him; she was smiling, but her expression was one of utter sadness. The 'spirit' looked so life-like that he cried out 'Hello.' She must have stood there a full minute. He got up from his fireside chair and walked towards her without any sense of terror or even a feeling of mild apprehension. When he was within a few feet of her she vanished.

A few nights later he awoke from sleep to see the same 'spirit' standing silhouetted against his bedroom window. She again looked at him with the same sad smile. She was so beautiful, her golden hair hanging over her shoulders, and all enhanced by the pale moonlight shining through the window. When she moved towards his bed he stretched out a hand to touch her, but she vanished.

Badger Hall was one of those great red brick mansions quite common in parts of Shropshire, and after the death of the last squire it was demolished. The squire was a well-liked person, highly esteemed by the villagers, and it was his custom to invite them to a Christmas Eve party. To the squire everyone was an equal, his motto being, 'We are all God's creatures.'

One particular party stands out quite vividly in the memory of my informant. The Hall had been beautifully decorated and after dinner there was plenty of dancing and merrymaking. Our story-teller was not particularly fond of dancing but preferred to chat with old friends. He was talking to some of them when a dance ended and the time was close on midnight. He had walked to the far end of the hall to get a drink and in doing so glanced at the door by a temporary stage where musicians were tuning up for the next dance, and there by the door stood the Grey Lady looking exactly as she had done on the two previous occasions, fascinatingly beautiful, but still very sad. He remembers the clock chiming the midnight hour as the 'spirit' moved across the hall towards him, and he could even hear a faint rustling as she glided along the floor. Everyone in the room saw her, the laughter ceased, a girl shouted, and then silence.

The gentle 'spirit' had crossed the room and was now close to him. He could see her sad luminous eyes and parted lips – she seemed to be trying to say something to him, something that would help take away the burden of sorrow she was carrying. Everyone in the hall was looking in his direction. He tried to speak but found that he could not utter a word. It was as if she had cast a spell over him. Again he stretched out his hand to touch her and, as before, she vanished. Instantly he was surrounded by friends who asked him if he had been afraid. 'She is quite harmless,' he told them, and he believes that the coolness he displayed helped to restore the party to its former gaiety.

He did not see the Grey Lady again until some years later. The squire had died, the Hall had been pulled down. Again it was a Christmas Eve and he walked through the ruins. He was recapturing pleasant memories of former years, reliving those happy times at the Hall. The night was very peaceful and a half-moon shone on the desolate and eerie scene. He felt as if part of his life lay among the ruins.

As he walked through the broken masonry he noticed the figure of a woman coming towards him. As she approached he at once recognised her as the Grey Lady. She was as beautiful as ever. When she was within a few feet of him she gave that same sad smile which had been so noticeable before. She seemed to be looking for something as if she could not rest until it was found. Suddenly she vanished, and from that day to this he has not seen the Grey Lady again. There is, however, a sequel to the story which may have some bearing on the reason why she has not been seen again.

Years afterwards some workmen were digging among the foundations of the Hall when they discovered an ancient and beautiful jewel box. It contained some valuable gems, among which was an engagement ring. Could it be that the lady had suffered a disappointment in love, perhaps a broken engagement, an act of infidelity?

Staffordshire

A Bloodstain and an Apparition

The Civil War in England was bloody. Many injustices, crimes and even murders were perpetrated in the name of religion; a blot on the life of the Church which no amount of theorising can eradicate. Puritanical fervour was at its zenith and many were the mockeries of trials brought about in the name of justice and God.

True, there was much corruption in the establishment and the priesthood was not held in high esteem by the majority of people, but the reprisals taken by fanatical Puritans in an attempt to 'cleanse the nation' were often cruel in the extreme. It is not surprising, therefore, that some houses and castle, now 'the ruins that Cromwell knocked about a bit', have their stories of brutality and tragedy.

Not far from Eccleshall in Staffordshire is Broughton Hall. It was probably Elizabethan, but it was restored and extended by Thomas Broughton whose initials T.B. appear on the left-hand side of the old front door. In this door is a hole said to be a bullet-hole. The story is that one of the Broughton heirs when entering the house was shot at by a hired assassin from a tree.

Throughout the centuries it has had a chequered history, and the story of its haunting takes us back to the time of the Civil War.

The story concerns a young heir of Broughton Hall, as fanatically for the King and the Royalist cause as were the Puritans for their desire to see an end to ritual within the church. He was standing in the Long Gallery on an upper floor when he saw a group of horsemen approaching. He recognised them as Roundhead troops and immediately the zeal of the Royalist youth was galvanised into activity. He flung open one of the windows and with an audacity beyond his years shouted down to the horsemen, 'I am for the King.' His reply was a bullet from a musket.

The boy was mortally wounded but managed to drag himself to a nearby room where he subsequently died. The wound was a severe one and he quickly lost a great deal of blood. Today the stain is still there on the floorboards of the Long Gallery and no amount of cleaning has been able to remove this reminder of the past.

Since that day people have seen the ghost of a young man, whom they have aptly named 'Red Socks' or 'Red Stockings' on account of the red hose he is seen to be wearing and one presumes he was wearing at the time of his death. The apparition has been seen standing in the Long Gallery looking out of the window, but on other occasions he has been seen walking down the Long Gallery and also descending the staircase.

Not far away from Broughton Hall stands Charnes Manor. This place too has a ghost, but for the moment we must leave this and mention the fact that the families of Charnes and Broughton Hall intermingled through marriage. Parties and celebrations were held in both places.

A story is told by a Miss Yonge of Charnes Manor who, about one hundred years ago, was invited to a party. The following is a written account of an experience she had while she was there.

'While playing hide and seek at Broughton, I went up into the Long Gallery to hide and crept behind the door of the first room on the left. After a few minutes I heard footsteps coming down the staircase which leads from the attic and waited for what seemed a very long time for the seeker to find my hiding place. As nothing happened, I ventured out into the Long Gallery and saw a young man, with red stockings, looking out of the window. I took him to be one of the sons of the house, who always wore knickerbockers and thick stockings. As he had his back to me, I thought, "This is my chance to get home without being seen", so I crept quietly past him and rushed down the stairs into the den where everyone was having tea. There, to my astonishment, was the son of the house sitting at the table, so I went up to him, smacked his knee and said, "However did you get down before me? I left you in the Long Gallery and you did not pass me on the stairs." The young boy seemed much bewildered and said, "You could not have seen me as I have not been up in the Long Gallery this afternoon." I had such an argument with him that the rest of the party stopped their tea to listen, and my hostess, thinking that my story was causing too much attention, took me by the hand and led me to the other end of the table, where I soon forgot all about the figure I had seen.'

Who was the figure in the Long Gallery? It seems quite likely that it was the spirit of the long dead heir. From all accounts, the lad was passionately fond of his home. Perhaps even today his spirit cannot leave the place to which he had formed so deep an attachment.

Another encounter with 'Red Stockings' is of a more recent date and concerns a woman from Fair Oak who was in domestic service at the Hall. One day she was scrubbing the stairs which lead to the attic from the Long Gallery. While she was busily engaged in her chores she became conscious of a presence, as though someone was near her. As far as she knew she was alone in that part of the house. She looked up and there at the top of the stairs stood a young man. He made no movement, but the look on his face indicated that he wanted to descend the stairs and the woman, thinking that she was in his way, moved her bucket to one side and stood up to let the boy pass. The figure then began to move down the steps, but it made straight for her, keeping close to the wall. Surely he would avoid the pail. But on he came and to her horror he walked right through her. One can imagine her fright, and she refused absolutely to clean the stairs afterwards. However, gentle persuasion changed her mind, but only on the condition that when she was in that part of the Hall someone was with her.

I do not know whether the figure of 'Red Stockings' has been seen recently, but certainly members of the families of Broughton Hall and Charnes Manor have had glimpses of him.

The Hall has, so far, escaped modern intrusions, long may it do so, and the restless spirit of the Broughton heir may yet walk the Long Gallery, happy to remain within the precincts of such a fine building.

A Dead Daughter

I have discovered that it is by no means uncommon for people who have lost relatives to believe that they are in communication with the departed. Sometimes it is, I am certain, imagination, or a guilt complex which periodically makes them succumb to hallucinations, or it may be that the person concerned is in need of some psychiatric treatment. The answers to some of the questions raised by such experiences are not always in the realm of the supernatural, although the person concerned is certain that these happenings, because of their vividness, are nothing less than an incursion into the spirit world. Be that as it may, I am well aware that science, medicine and certain branches of psychiatry can be therapeutic in their treatment.

But there are certain experiences which people have that cannot be explained by scientific and rational conclusions.

Towards the end of 1969 I was invited to the house of a Mrs W. To say that she lives in Staffordshire is sufficient, and if this sounds as though I am being evasive about her identity and actual residence, it is because I do not wish her to be 'invaded' by prying folk who, for reasons best known to themselves, get a kick out of delving into the private and often very personal experiences of others.

At this point I must say that Mrs W gave me full permission to use her name and address, but I have withheld them for reasons stated above. When she knew that my investigations were not just the work of a sensation-hunter, but that I was prepared to treat her experiences seriously, then she volunteered what follows.

Mrs W's daughter, Audrey, died in 1954 from leukaemia. She was married, with a boy who was then two years old. Mrs W was aware of her daughter's condition and knew that it was only a matter of time before she would die. Only those people in similar positions know the agony through which the mind passes, realising that the death of a loved one is inevitable.

Eventually she died, but since her death Mrs W has had some very unusual experiences which have, on most occasions, left her feeling quite ill and sometimes in a mild state of shock.

I interviewed this quietly spoken lady who told me in quite unemotional terms how she has, on a number of occasions, seen her dead daughter. The first time this happened was a few years ago. She was ironing in the neat little kitchen of her council house and she had no thoughts in her mind other than the work in hand. Quite suddenly she knew that someone was coming down the stairs, but just who it was she didn't know, for the house was empty, the rest of the family being out at work. She placed her iron on the board and walked to the small entrance hall. Suddenly a picture came off the wall; it didn't just fall from the hook on which it hung, but it came from the wall as though flung outwards by some unseen hand, and then to her terror she saw the figure of her dead daughter at the foot of the stairs. She turned and came towards her mother, looking straight ahead all the time. Mrs W began to feel very faint and clung to the wall for support. This experience affected her badly and the doctor had to be called.

Later that night three very loud knocks were heard at the front door. The dog responded in its usual way by barking loudly, but when Mrs W opened the door there was no one to be seen. Within half an hour of the knocks, Mrs W, who was standing by the window, saw her brother walking up the garden path. He did not speak at first, but just stood there silent and obviously at a loss for words. Eventually he blurted out that their mother had died at half past two that afternoon, the exact time when her daughter appeared.

Other strange happenings have taken place also. One time when Mrs W visited the grave of her daughter she was aware of a mist slowly rising from the ground; it had no particular shape, but it hovered over the place for a few seconds and then disappeared.

Now one might feel that these appearances were the result of a distraught mind; that they were merely hallucinations brought on by the tragedy of the event; at first I thought that this could well be the cause, but a subsequent account concerning one of her other married daughters led me to change my mind.

In 1966, the other married daughter gave birth to a baby girl, but she had a most difficult labour and in the end she had to have a Caesarean operation, for the unborn child was at great risk and this was the only hope of survival. After the operation the girl heard her dead sister's voice saying, 'It's all over now, you will be all right.' Then she felt a cool hand pass over her forehead. The mother spoke to her dead sister, but cannot remember exactly what she said.

One of the nurses on duty asked her to whom she was speaking, and wanted to know who was in with her for she had heard the mother's name mentioned. She asked if the baby was living, secretly she feared that the child was stillborn, but the nurse replied that she had a fine bouncing girl.

When Mrs W visited her sick daughter in hospital, her daughter told her about the experience of speaking to her sister. Now Mrs W distinctly remembers the words she said to her when she was alive and was due to give birth to a child. She too had a difficult birth and kept shouting. When it was all over and the child was born, a son mentioned previously, Mrs W said, 'It's all over now, you will be all right', the exact words spoken by the dead sister.

Mrs W's daughter quite frequently appears to her mother in the bedroom at night. At first Mrs W believed that it was a dream, but she realised that she was fully conscious and aware of her surroundings. She remembers one occasion when her daughter appeared, for she had an overwhelming feeling of foreboding as though some awful event was imminent. The following morning she told the rest of the family that one of her sons had been involved in a crash; this was at twelve noon. The other daughters and another son were inclined to laugh at this until later in the day the boy was brought home by a workmate. His car had skidded on a patch of black ice and turned over and he had sustained injuries to his head and back. The accident took place at exactly twelve noon, the time Mrs W had said it had happened. She is quite convinced that the appearance of her dead daughter often precedes an unpleasant event, not always a death, but a happening which is considered with no small amount of apprehension.

Often Mrs W herself has been taken ill after she has seen her daughter. It is as though she serves as a warning. Now why should the daughter keep appearing in this way? Is it just a figment of Mrs W's imagination on account of her loss or is it something deeper than that?

I do not think that a supernatural manifestation can be ruled out entirely. The case poses many problems, some of which would, no doubt, be of interest to the medical profession, but I do not think they could supply conclusive answers. I myself was impressed by the way in which Mrs W told her story. She herself firmly believes that her daughter does come back from the dead, that for some reason she is earthbound. There was great love between mother and daughter and that bond is unbroken by death.

A Incident on the Rugeley Road

In September 1969, I received the following letter from Mr Wilfred Daniels, a mechanical engineer, of Stafford. The letter relates to a very strange incident which happened as he was motoring south to spend his holidays with his sister, Miss Dorothy Daniels, in Sussex, and I can do no better than quote Mr Daniels' letter.

'In June 1949 I left 340 Oxford Gardens, Stafford, at approximately 6.00 a.m., for Seaford, Sussex, on a two weeks' holiday with my wife Violet Irene and our (then) baby son, Michael, aged two. We were in a 1934 "Standard 9" 4-door saloon car, my wife in the front passenger seat beside me, the baby boy on his mother's knee.

'After passing through Milford en route for Lichfield, the car topped the last rise on that road and levelled off on the stretch past the fringe of woods taking in Weetmans Bridge to the left as one travels south.

'The road was now empty, save for a biggish fellow on a bicycle riding towards Rugeley, who came into view as the car topped that last, gentle rise. He was dressed in what appeared to be jacket and trousers of black, heavy serge and he was pressing along steadily on a high-framed bicycle of a rather dated style.

'I eased the car towards the road centre to do a normal overtake, giving him instinctively the normal amount of clearance, and was just about bonnet-to-back-wheel level with him when, with an overwhelming sense of appalling shock, I saw the road *empty* of all save my own car.

'My back hair bristled, my entire scalp "crawled", my spine had crushed ice slithering down it; in good daylight, at about 6.25 a.m., I had seen the "impossible" – a solid figure pedalling a solid bicycle had vanished before my eyes.

'I turned to my wife and said in an awkward fashion, "Did you see a man on a bike?" Her face as white as chalk, she turned very slowly, searching my face, and said in a shocked whisper, "Well . . . I thought I did." "Yes", I replied, "and I thought I did", and drove on.

'That afternoon, as we took a cup of tea after arriving at my younger sister's flat (she lived at that time at Chichester Lodge, Claremont Road, Seaford, Sussex), I told her the story.

'Miss Dorothy Daniels gazed unseeingly into infinity for a few seconds and then said, "Did you know that stretch of Lichfield Road is supposed to be haunted?"

' "No!" I replied.

' "No", said she, "I don't suppose you would, as you were only a child at the time, but years ago there was an accident along there and ever since the place has reckoned to be haunted."

'Back at work in the former Research Drawing Office, English Electric, Stafford, I recounted all the foregoing to a colleague, Jim Walker, who lived then at Great Haywood, about two miles to the east of the ill-reputed stretch of Lichfield Road. My astonishment may be imagined when he said, "Your sister is quite right, and I can tell you what happened. It was when the water engineers were doing the pumping station that stands in the ornamental walled garden on the right-hand side nearly opposite the lane down to Weetmans Bridge. There was a deep shaft, a vertical bore-hole, and one morning, just after the men had started work, one of them fell down the shaft and was choked to death at the bottom, and I can tell you who fetched the poor b—— up. It was Chief Fire Officer Coglan, but of course he was only an ordinary fireman in those days. He volunteered to go down in a bucket and brought him up. And ever since then, that piece of road has been declared to be haunted."

'All I know beyond all shadow of doubt is that my wife and I both saw a man, and on a bicycle to boot, who, in less than a split second, just wasn't there.'

The above account is signed as a true statement by Mr Daniels. It is indeed, to say the least, an unusual story, but his experience is not a unique one. Not far from Eccleshall there is a stretch of road known as 'Ghost Mile' and many people have said that they have seen the figure of a man dressed in Tudor costume glide across the road. On one occasion a young accountant driving home on a winter's evening saw someone dash out of the hedge right in front of his car. There was no time to apply the brakes to avoid an accident, and the car ran right into the figure. The young man got out of his car expecting to find the twisted body of a man on the road, but found nothing. There were no marks on his car which indicated a bump and on reflection he realised that there had in fact been no impact. The experience quite unnerved him and he arrived home in a state of shock.

Mr Daniels is regarded in this country as an Unidentified Flying Objects expert, and his investigations are carried out with meticulous care for detail. I have heard him broadcast on the subject and my impression is that he is one of the most rational of men, not given to over-imagination; in fact quite the reverse. His approach to his subject is a scientific one.

Note the fact that both he and his wife experienced the disappearance. Did the figure on the bicycle not wish to be recognised, for it was just at the time when Mr Daniels was about to pull in front of the figure that it vanished? Note also that Mr Daniels observed that the bicycle the man was riding was an old and somewhat outdated model; this would bring it in line with the time the accident took place. Neither was aware that that particular stretch of road was reputed to be haunted, so there is nothing to suggest that they were influenced by a pre-knowledge of the spectre.

The man involved in the accident met a violent death, with a terrible prelude. But why does he ride his bicycle? Is he trying to escape the tragedy, but cannot? In most instances of hauntings the apparitions are of the departed who have suffered some form of tragedy while living.

It would be mere speculation and presumption to attempt to provide satisfactory and conclusive reasons for such a manifestation – but such events witnessed by rational people cannot be lightly ignored.

Checkley Rectory

I was working on some project for the church to undertake, when the telephone rang and a very pleasant voice asked, 'Is that the Reverend Travis who's wanting to know about ghosts and such like?' I answered that it was and I would be very interested to listen to what he had to say. The ensuing conversation revealed that I was speaking to a man who was widely read and exceptionally well versed in local folklore.

Mr Walker lives at Tean in North Staffordshire and has a deep interest in local history. Being a prodigious reader, he has accumulated a wealth of knowledge, which makes him a person well worth listening to.

He asked me if I had heard about the haunting of Checkley Rectory and when I told him that I had not, he went into great detail, giving names of people, dates and other relevant information which, on subsequent investigation, showed considerable accuracy. Right from the beginning of the conversation I was interested and as he went along, relating more details, my enthusiasm was well and truly fired.

The story of the haunting of Checkley Rectory has led me to meet quite a number of people and from my discussions with them I am of the opinion that this is one of the most authentic cases of a haunting which I have investigated. I have endeavoured to leave no stone unturned in my digging into the past and my conclusion is that Checkley Rectory is haunted, and that the hauntings are not entirely confined to the building. Far from it.

It was in 1878 that the Rector of Checkley, the Rev. William Hutchinson, died and left a widow. The rectory was then situated about half a mile away from the church and parts of it date back many centuries. Today it is a large farmhouse, but it is not this house with which we are concerned but another property, much nearer the church and of a smaller size than the original rectory.

After Hutchinson's death the large and rambling building was sold and Mrs Hutchinson moved into the new rectory much nearer the church and, as the next incumbent lived in a nearby village, she was allowed to stay there until her death in 1895.

It is said that Mrs Hutchinson ruled the parish with a rod of iron and that there was little she missed. Absentees from church were often called on by the rector's wife and were told in no uncertain terms that they had no business to stay away. It seems that she crossed swords with a number of people, especially with a family who lived in the house which was later bought as the next rectory and where she spent the remainder of her life.

The family who lived there had a rather bad reputation. There were some high-spirited girls who frequently rode their horses across the churchyard and among the gravestones, not caring about the damage they did, nor about the desecration of consecrated ground. Mrs Hutchinson was naturally furious and there was considerable enmity between them.

It is quite possible that the family who lived in the house ran a small private boarding school, but I cannot find definite proof of this, though the present rector believes that this was so. If it were, then it would probably have added fuel to the fires of bitterness, because very shortly after the death of Mr Hutchinson, a Church of England school was built to his memory. It is still known as the Hutchinson Memorial School. It may well have been that there was some jealousy on account of the competition between the two schools which were less than one hundred yards from each other.

Eventually the family moved out of the house and it was bought and became the new rectory. It is this building which is said to be haunted by the ghost of Mrs Hutchinson.

The present rector's predecessor, the Rev. Ralph Philips, died in 1966, but when he moved into the rectory over twenty years ago he decided that he would have a house warming. All the guests, with one exception, arrived in the afternoon or early evening. The Rev. David Hemming did not reach the rectory until very late. Mrs Philips waited up for him and after having given him a meal went to bed. Mr Hemming later went to his bedroom and when he had gone to bed he discovered that there was no clock in the room. It was essential that he should know the time because he had promised the rector that he would take the early morning service. He remembered that he had a pocket watch in his coat which he had left in the hall, so there was nothing left but to go downstairs and get it. He fumbled his way along the landing and down the wide staircase until he reached the place where he had left his coat. He took out the watch and turned to ascend the stairs. As he put his foot on the bottom stair he saw, half-way up the staircase, the figure of an old lady dressed in old-fashioned black clothes and what appeared to be a white mob cap; she was carrying a stick and there was a dog beside her.

Hemming was about to call out but thought that it was one of the guests, so he went back to bed and slept peacefully.

In the morning when all the guests were at breakfast Mr Philips introduced Mr Hemming to the others. After he had been at the table for a few minutes Mr Hemming asked the whereabouts of the old lady and why she wasn't at breakfast. The rector asked his questioner what he meant. Mr Hemming related his experience during the early hours of that morning. A smile spread across the face of the rector, who said, 'Oh, the old lady, well you won't see her at breakfast. The person you saw was the ghost of Mrs Hutchinson.'

The rector and his wife on more than one occasion saw this apparition and also heard a voice. One morning Mrs Philips was in the kitchen when she heard her name being called. The voice came from the top of the stairs and it was calling her by her Christian name. Thinking it was her husband, she went to the foot of the stairs, but saw no one. She called out in answer, but got no reply. This happened two or three times during the morning. She had been alone in the house, not knowing that the rector had gone out.

Some months later both the rector and his wife heard their names called from somewhere upstairs, as if there was someone on the landing. They both quickly went to the foot of the stairs and were just in time to see the figure of an old lady wearing long flowing black cloth and a white mob cap, carrying a stick and walking soundlessly up the stairs. By her side was a little white dog. The old lady and the dog walked through a closed door of one of the bedrooms.

During a parish council meeting which was held in the rectory there were three loud knocks at the door of the large room in which the meeting was being held. One of the members got up from her chair and opened the door only to discover that there was no one there. These knocks were heard again a few minutes later and again when the door was opened no one was there. The rector said that it must be Mrs Hutchinson, for he never quite knew when and where she would appear and what she would do.

It seems that this particular apparition was quite innocuous and was accepted by the Philipses as one of the family; certainly there was no atmosphere of fear about the place.

I decided that I really ought to go and talk to the present rector. The Rev. George Lawton and his wife have been at Checkley since 1959 and on my arrival they made me most welcome and were extremely helpful. I was shown into Mr Lawton's study and there I remained for a little while until Mr Lawton arrived. During those few minutes while I was alone in the study I had an uneasy feeling that I was being watched by someone or something that was quite indefinable. I am not a nervous person but I was certainly not at ease in that study. There was nothing unusual about the room; it was like most ministers' studies, with hundreds of books piled high on shelves reaching to the ceiling. I was quite glad when Mr Lawton appeared with his wife.

Mrs Lawton told me that she had been in the village only a few days after their arrival in 1959 when she was stopped by someone in the post office who said that she wouldn't live in the place. Mrs Lawton, somewhat taken aback, asked her why not, and the woman replied saying that the rectory was haunted. Mrs Lawton laughed at the idea, but as time went on she heard more and more about the ghost of Mrs Hutchinson.

Mr Lawton considers himself a rationalist and he took little notice of these stories. I asked if either of them had seen the ghost; they had not, but on several occasions they had definitely heard footsteps on the upstairs landing and had been absolutely convinced that someone other than themselves had been in the house. So certain were they on one occasion that a nocturnal visitor was walking about that they got up in the very early hours and searched every room – but found nothing.

It must be stated that after the Lawtons had been in the rectory for a year extensive alterations were made and a considerable part of the original staircase – a favourite spot for the appearance of the ghost – was taken away.

But Mrs Hutchinson does not confine herself to the rectory; she has appeared at the school which was built in memory of her husband. Mr Lawton took me there and introduced me to the headmistress, Miss K. M. Hollins, who related a very unusual experience.

She lives in a detached house next to the school playground, so it takes only a few seconds to get to the school building. Miss Hollins had heard of the ghost, but was sceptical. At that time there was a Mrs Fairbanks who was the school caretaker and often used to work in the dusk, to save electricity, as she cleared the classrooms.

Miss Hollins wanted some books which she had left in one of the school rooms, so at about five o'clock she left her house and went into the school building. There were no lights burning, but she did not think this unusual, knowing Mrs Fairbanks's careful habits. She opened the door of the room in which she had left the books and as she took them from off the table she noticed a figure at the far end of the room. It was the figure of a woman who appeared to be wearing dark clothes and something white on her head. Because of the poor light it was difficult to identify it and as the figure appeared to be making sweeping movements Miss Hollins assumed that it was the caretaker.

When she left the room and was only a few paces down the passage leading to the door she turned back to switch on the electric light because she felt that Mrs Fairbanks could not see well enough to do her work properly. She switched on the light, and was about to say something when she saw that there was no one in the room. She then searched the rest of the school, but she was alone. In the space of a few seconds the person had vanished. The next day Miss Hollins asked Mrs Fairbanks why she had worked in the dark and where had she gone when the light had been switched on. You can imagine her surprise when the caretaker said that she had not been near the school all day!

I have had conversations with Miss Hollins' predecessor, Miss Stonehouse, who was the headmistress from April 1935 to April 1939. She too had an unusual experience, not only with the ghost of Mrs Hutchinson but also that of a monk.

It was an early Monday evening in the spring of 1939 when

Miss Stonehouse was sitting at a table in her sitting-room preparing work for the coming day. This was in the School House at Checkley, next door to the Hutchinson Memorial Church of England School, the playground separating the two buildings.

From where she sat she could see everyone who came through the school gates, her attention always attracted by the click of the latch. On this evening, when the daylight was drawing in, she noticed the figure of a little old lady dressed in a mob cap and a grey alpaca gown reaching down to the top of her shoes. A woollen waistcoat framed a white ruched front, her hair was grey under the mob cap. Who could she be? Miss Stonehouse felt strangely cold. Perhaps, she thought, it was someone visiting her housekeeper. It was a strange thing that she had not on this occasion heard the click of the latch on the gate, but there was the old lady in the middle of the playground. The old lady did not look at her, but Miss Stonehouse paid little attention, as her housekeeper's visitors did not disturb her and usually went to the back door.

Passing beyond the window, the old lady must have gone in because she did not come back that way. Later Mrs Pillans, the housekeeper, brought Miss Stonehouse's supper tray and was asked about her visitor. The housekeeper, quite surprised by this question, said that she had not had a visitor at all that night but had spent most of her time ironing in her room at the back of the house. The old lady was described to Mrs Pillans, who said that the description did not fit anyone she knew.

The next morning, she remembered the old lady and described her to another mistress at the school. She smiled, but before she could explain the Rev. Drinkwater, then rector of Checkley, arrived to take morning prayers. Mrs Collier spoke to the rector in an excited manner, saying that Miss Stonehouse had seen Mrs Hutchinson. The rector replied by saying that it wouldn't be long before Miss Stonehouse left. Mr Frost, the first headmaster of the school, had seen her after thirty-five years and his successor, Miss Wilkinson, after a few years. Both left not long after. Was it just coincidence that later in the year Miss Stonehouse accepted the post of headmistress at a school in Uttoxeter?

The following day Miss Stonehouse went to see the rector. While she was waiting for him at the rectory she saw a picture of the person she had seen in the school playground. When he came in he said, 'So you have seen the ghost of Mrs Hutchinson after all.' This was the only time that Miss Stonehouse saw Mrs Hutchinson.

Another strange and very disturbing incident happened to Miss Stonehouse during one Sunday evening in winter. No one ever crossed the churchyard, a short cut to the School House, at night. In a hurry to get home that particular evening, she decided to cross the churchyard in the dark. She had crossed it daily in daylight and knew every twist and turn. She started out but was stopped half-way. Fear began to grip her; she tried to press on, but something held her back. At one point she thought that she had come up against a headstone or even a tree but she could not discern any shape. Still the force held her back and she returned to the church and home by the road. The next day she went across the churchyard but found no tree or obstacle in her path.

There is great difficulty in getting grave-diggers to work in the Checkley churchyard, not because of labour shortage but because they don't like the atmosphere; they feel that someone unseen is watching them.

During her time at Checkley, Miss Stonehouse had the rector's permission to play the church organ, which she did frequently. When she had finished she would go to the church tower to turn off the lights and would then grope her way back to the north door, lock it and leave the key at the rectory. She never had the slightest fear, the church always felt so very friendly, but once or twice she thought that she could see a hooded figure near the altar as she stood at the other end of the church. Whatever it was, she was unafraid, thinking it was perhaps a trick of light through the window. But was it the Abbot of Croxden, whose grave was in the chancel, side by side with that of the usurpers of his abbey, the Foljambes? The rector told her that he often saw the figure of a hooded monk slipping into the shadows when he was in church.

The old postmistress who used to arrange the flowers said that she too had often seen the monk and, when she became too old to do the job, her daughter-in-law who took her place also saw the hooded figure. No one who had seen him felt that he was anything but friendly.

On one occasion the ghost of a little white dog has been seen by itself. A lady in the village had come to make an appointment with one of the previous rectors and while she was waiting in the entrance hall she saw the dog walk in front of her; she left the rectory in a great hurry, not waiting to see the rector, and vowed never again to enter the place.

Elford Rectory

About three miles north of Tamworth in Staffordshire is the small village of Elford, four miles due west is ancient Lichfield. In 1966 Elford Hall was demolished and in the early 1950s the rectory was sold and is now a private residence. It is the original rectory with which we are concerned, for there is recorded in a letter written in 1877 by the Rev. Francis Paget, the rector, a very strange and what can only be determined as a supernatural experience. Paget was a man of some standing in the village and his son became the squire and lived in the Hall which was next to the rectory.

The letter refers to the appearance of a very close friend of the rector. The words which follow are in fact the full context of what he wrote.

'In the house in which these pages are written a tall and wide staircase window, with a southern aspect, throws a strong side light on to the entrance in the chief living-room, which stands at the end of a passage running nearly the length of the house. It was after midday in mid-winter many years since, that the writer left his study, which opens into the passage just mentioned, on his way to his early dinner. The day was rather foggy, but there was no density of vapour, yet the door at the end of the passage seemed obscured in mist; as he advanced, the mist (so to call it) gathered into one spot, deepened, and formed itself into the outline of a human figure, the head and shoulders becoming more and more distinct while the rest of the body seemed enveloped in a gauzy cloak, like a vestment of many folds, reaching downwards so as to hide the feet and from its width as it rested on the flagged passage giving a pyramidical outline. The full light of the window fell on this object, which was so thin and tenuous in its consistency, that the light on the panels of a highly varnished door were visible through the lower part of the dress. It was altogether colourless – a statue carved in mist.

'The writer was so startled that he is uncertain whether he moved forward or stood still. He was more astonished than terrified, for his first notion was that he was witnessing some hitherto unnoticed effect of light and shade. He had no thought of anything supernatural till, as he gazed, the head was turned towards him, and he at once recognised the features of a very dear friend. The expression of his countenance was that of holy, peaceful repose, and the gentle kindly aspect it wore in daily life was intensified (so the writer, in recalling the sight, has ever since felt) into a parting glance of deep affection; and then, in an instant all passed away.

'The writer can only compare the manner of the evanescence to the way in which a jet of steam is dissipated on exposure to cold air. Hardly, till then, did he realise that he had been brought into close contact with the supernatural. The result was great awe, but no terror; so that, instead of retreating to his study, he went forward and opened the door, close to which the apparition had stood. Of course, he could not doubt the impact of what he had seen, and the morrow or the next day's post brought the tidings that his friend had tranquilly passed out of this world at the time when he was seen by the writer. It must be stated that it was a sudden summons, that the writer had heard nothing of him for some weeks previously, and that nothing had brought him to his thoughts on the day of his decease. The writer never crosses the spot where the figure stood, but imagination reproduces the scene, but it has no element of fear.

Elford Rectory, 1877.'

The experience of the Rev. Francis Paget is certainly unusual, but it is not unique. The appearance to others at the time of death of those who have died, especially if they are relatives or where there has been a deep bond of attachment, has been recorded by a number of people. Notice that the rector experienced no fear and was not in any way considering the forces of the supernatural—indeed he thought that it was some trick of light which had not been seen before.

Some years ago there was a similar case in which a young woman, while cleaning her cottage, happened to look out of the window and walking up the garden path, dressed in naval officer's uniform, was her brother. His appearance evoked surprise and considerable joy, because she believed he was still on active service. Perhaps he had come to make the visit so that it would be a happy surprise. She rushed to the door and flung it open and called out his name, 'John', but there was no one to be seen. A thorough search of the garden revealed nothing at all.

A few days after this incident the woman received a letter from the Admiralty informing her that her brother had been killed in action while at sea. The date and time fitted exactly with the appearance of the dead brother. Subsequent information revealed that there was great affection between brother and sister and she afterwards concluded that he had come to tell her of his departure from this world. Although his death in action was tragic, the sister was satisfied that he lived on; perhaps he had come to tell her that they would be reunited in time to come.

This leads me to another, but more disturbing, explanation of the appearance of the departed to close friends. Some people have made pacts that whoever is first to die shall show himself to the other to prove the existence of life beyond the grave. Again there are well-authenticated stories of this actually happening. One eminent person made such a pact with a friend and his appearance preceded notification of his death. It was the sealing of the bond made between them.

A more sinister form of trying to contact the dead is that of raising them from their resting places. Many have tried, many have failed, some have succeeded and some of those who have done so have either gone insane or died. Elliott O'Donnell records a number of such cases, especially that of a sceptical and rather cynical undergraduate. He decided, for the hell of it, to gather a few of his undergraduate friends together in a deserted and reportedly haunted house and so attempt to raise the spirit of the departed. To his horror, he succeeded. Some of the assembled students fled in panic and great terror, others fainted, whilst he himself never recovered and was admitted to a lunatic asylum.

These experiences of men and women add weight to the belief in life after death and, after all, why shouldn't the wraiths of dear friends attempt to communicate with those who still live – they don't come to strike terror, but to assure them that beyond the grave there is life.

Not all such manifestations are malevolent and evil. The bond of affection, deepened by years of friendship, does not come to an end with death; it remains. Who can tell what strength, what force there is in human relationships, a strength that reveals itself beyond the tomb? The dead are not always to be feared.

He Came to Warn

It is strange how members of a family can be warned of impending danger and even death. Some people seem to possess what is commonly known as a sixth sense sometimes referred to as extrasensory perception. They just know that something is going to happen or they have a feeling that something has in fact taken place. Such prophetic insight remains a mystery and theories put forward to offer explanations are all inconclusive, and some are no more than speculative.

There are events which, if not foretold, are indicated by the presence of the departed and it has been made quite obvious to me that the dead do return to show that death is imminent. Such have been the experiences of a Mrs Allen who lives in Cheadle, Staffordshire. Not only has Mrs Allen felt the presence of someone or something unknown and frightening, but one of her sons and a daughter have actually seen the ghost of a previous occupant of the house in which they lived.

The house has a reputation for being haunted and people who know something of its history will have nothing to do with it. Of course Mrs Allen realises that the events which took place in the house, many of them confirmed by her children, are regarded by some people as just imagination, but she is absolutely convinced that the supernatural was at work there. The spirit was not an evil force although its appearance evoked some fear in the family.

Mrs Allen's grandmother lived in the house for over forty years and she too was aware of a presence, but it did not upset her in any way, for she regarded the wraith as quite harmless, but its appearance did promote a feeling of apprehension, because each time it revealed itself it was an unmistakable sign of danger or death.

Before Mrs Allen's grandmother lived in the house, there used to be a Joseph Ambrose Pyatt who lived there and who also died in the house. His grave and headstone are situated in an old part of Cheadle cemetery near an old chapel. It is the ghost of this old man which haunts the house.

Mrs Allen remembers as a girl of twelve peeping through the scullery window at a spiritualist medium who had been called in to see if it could be discovered why the old man's spirit was still tied to the house. After a seance the medium told the family that there was something in the house which the old man was looking for and he could not rest until it was found, but that he would not harm the children.

Mrs Allen lived with her grandparents from 1942–1946 but she never actually saw the old man, though she had the feeling that whenever she was upstairs she was not alone; it was as though someone was watching her every move. When she referred to this 'strange feeling' her grandmother would say quite jovially, 'It's only old Ammy, the dead won't hurt you, it's only the living who do that.'

When her grandmother was ill her son Patrick was invited to stay in the house. One night when he was in bed he saw the old man and his description fitted him exactly as he was when alive. Of course, the boy was frightened and would not stay in the house. Even today the boy does not like to speak of the experience because not only was it rather frightening, it was so vivid and he has not forgotten.

While the boy was lying in bed the figure of the old man slowly approached his bed and gently took hold of the bedclothes and covered him up, as though there was a parental fondness in the spirit, but the sight of a complete stranger in the house upset the child and he left for home the next day, refusing to return. A few days after his experience, a cousin of Mrs Allen's was buried alive in a pit disaster at Foxfield Colliery. Fortunately he was rescued. The medium who had seen Mrs Allen's grandmother had in fact pointed out that the appearance of the old man was foretelling trouble.

This happened on other occasions and the appearance was quickly followed by the deaths of Mrs Allen's father and brother. But the strangest event of all took place one evening when Mrs Allen was in bed. On this occasion she saw nothing, but experienced the most unusual sensations.

During February 1944, Mrs Allen was living with her grandmother. She had retired to bed at approximately ten forty-five and she lay in bed with her knees up. No particular thoughts were in her mind. She was gazing up at the ceiling when all at once she heard the purring of a cat. Quite suddenly she felt a weight on her chest and was convinced that the animal had jumped on the bed. She felt it slowly moving down her body. All the use went out of her limbs, she could not, to quote her, 'have bent her little finger'. Her head was full of noises, as though there were hundreds of steam engines banging away, and it felt as though her eardrums would burst. She felt the animal walk out from under her legs and immediately the use flowed back into her body.

With grim determination she jumped out of bed and switched on the light; the bedroom door was shut, as it had been after she first entered the room that night. She hunted under the bed, a chest of drawers, in all the corners of the room, searching for any place that a cat might hide itself – but there was nothing to be seen or heard. Whatever it was had simply disappeared into thin air.

The following morning she told her grandmother about her terrible experience and she replied, 'It would be Ammy', the rather affectionate name she had for the ghost, but she showed no small amount of concern because she knew that something unpleasant was going to happen. It happened a week later.

Mrs Allen received news that her husband had been wounded in Burma and had subsequently died.

A mystery remains – why, if it was the ghost of 'Ammy', didn't he actually appear to Mrs Allen? Her grandmother was quite convinced that the presence in the bedroom was the spirit of the dead man. The family do not very often speak of these strange manifestations, but to them they are very real. The benevolent spirit of the old man may still be about to warn of a forthcoming disaster – who knows? – only those who live in the house.

The House of Fear

Strange noises, moving furniture, footsteps on the stairs and ghostly visions, all these took place in a cottage at Longnor, a village on the Staffordshire-Derbyshire border. The disturbances became so violent that eventually the occupants had to leave the cottage and now live in Leek, about six miles away.

In 1960 the hauntings of this particular place were reported in the national press and much publicity ensued. Tape recordings were taken and one or two broadcasts were made; in fact, there were broadcasts in Canada about the house, such was the interest shown at that time.

I have been in contact with Mr Wood who lived in the cottage with his mother for many years and also Mrs Brittlebank, Mr Wood's cousin, who experienced some terrifying events when she came to nurse Mr Wood after his mother had died and who himself had been unwell.

In 1960 Mr Wood was admitted to a hospital in Stockport for an operation and while he was away from home his mother, an old lady of eighty, was taken seriously ill with a stroke. Mrs Brittlebank came to look after Mrs Wood, but after a week Mrs Wood herself was admitted to hospital, where she subsequently died.

When Mr Wood came out of hospital he lived alone, Mrs Brittlebank having returned home. It was some considerable time before he was able to resume work and for the first few weeks after his return he was in the house by himself for most of the time. He distinctly remembers the first unusual experience that happened to him. On 14th January 1961 he went to bed at about ten o'clock in the evening and was awakened in the early hours of the morning; there was someone or something in the room. He felt that an ice-cold hand was firmly gripping his, but thinking this might well be his imagination he thought little about the matter.

Some days later during the very early hours of the morning he was awakened by a loud noise. It sounded as though the handle of a bucket had been dropped down; it had a metallic ring to it and the noise came from the kitchen. Again he thought little about it, certainly he had no thoughts about the noise being caused by any supernatural force. But there was worse to come. The following evening as he reached the top of the stairs there was a deafening crash as though the ceiling in one of the bedrooms had collapsed, the sound of falling plaster lasting for quite a few seconds. Quite unnerved by this, he did not look in that bedroom until the following morning and when he did investigate he discovered that not a thing had been disturbed, no fallen ceiling, beams or plaster.

Eventually he could bear the place no longer and went to Leek, where he stayed with friends for a few days. They were inclined to be sceptical about such happenings, suggesting that it was his imagination.

After spending some time with his friends, he returned to the cottage feeling somewhat better for the break. He had been back a few weeks and nothing unusual happened until one day as he was sorting out some old papers there was a most fearful noise as numerous empty cartons came bumping down the stairs. No one else was in the cottage. Who had thrown them down the stairs?

Noises were not the only extraordinary happenings. Soon after the business of the cartons being hurled from the top of the stairs, Mr Wood saw something which gave him a considerable fright. He was lying in bed, quite wide awake, when he saw the latch of his bedroom door lift up. The door opened about twelve inches, then stopped as though held by some unseen hand. Slowly it began to move again until it was fully opened, and there, standing in the doorway, was the figure of an old lady. She was wearing a black dress and black cape and he noticed that she had silvery white hair. The figure walked towards the bed and then moved to one side and walked right through the wardrobe. Mr Wood was terrified by what he saw and says that could he have shouted out he would have done, but he could not utter a word, it seemed as though the last ounce of energy and strength had been drained from his body.

After this he did not sleep in the dark again, but had a darkened bulb in the room.

Mr Wood told me that the person who had sold the cottage to his mother years before had dropped hints about disturbances but little or no notice was taken of this. A man who had lived in the cottage before the woman bought it from him also related stories of unusual happenings; she too took little notice until one evening when she was sitting in front of the fire with her husband pegging a rug. She had pinned the rug to herself so that it would be kept straight and would not slip. The cat was lying on the hearth asleep, this being its favourite place in the cottage. Suddenly the animal fled under the settee and at the same time the rug was violently flung from the woman's knees and thrown into a corner of the room. The same rug remains unfinished to this day. After a time the couple moved out of the cottage to another one only two doors away and eventually the place was sold to Mrs Wood.

During the time of the disturbances some members of a psychic society were asked to investigate the cottage.

Through the help of a medium it was established that there was some force at work in the house and that the spirit was evil. It seems that it was an old man who had a dog and that the latter plays a significant part in these mysterious happenings.

After Mr Wood had come out of hospital he was thinking that he ought to try and do something to break the monotony, so he decided to pull up a flagstone in the doorway leading to the scullery. The stone was duly lifted and about ten inches of earth scooped out in preparation for replacing it with cement. As it was nearing evening he decided to complete the work the following day. He went outside to chop a few sticks for the next day.

His cousin, Mrs Brittlebank, was staying with him at this time in order to help him recover from his operation. She was going out of the living-room into the scullery when she suddenly froze to the spot. Out of the hole which Mr Wood had made by lifting the broken flagstone there appeared a dog. Mrs Brittlebank screamed and came to the door shouting for her cousin. He placed a board over the hole and covered it with a rug. There were no further appearances of the dog, but this by no means put an end to other experiences equally as alarming.

Under the staircase was a loose flagstone, and Mr Wood

decided to take it up and bed it in cement. The stone was lifted and replaced, a straightforward job, but there followed an event that Mrs Brittlebank remembers vividly. The following day she was climbing the stairs when she felt as though something was pushing her back and, whatever it was, it was standing directly above the place where the stone had been moved.

Again a medium was called in to see if help could be given and Mr Wood was told that in all probability a corpse was buried under the foundations of the cottage. Many years ago Longnor was a notorious area, wild and bleak, and a few people met violent ends at the hands of ruffians. The body of a person could have been hidden in those desolate parts centuries ago, long before there were any human habitations in the area. Could it be that this cottage was built over the body of an old man who had met a violent and cruel death? It is a sobering thought.

Today no one lives in the cottage, it is empty. There are a number of witnesses who can lay claim to strange happenings in that cottage, not least among them those who have lived there.

Now we must hear the testimony of Mrs Brittlebank who, you will remember, came to nurse Mrs Wood when she was ill after her son had been admitted to hospital. She had what she calls 'nerve racking experiences' which so greatly upset her that even today she cannot think of the place without a shudder.

When she went to stay with her aunt she slept in the same bedroom as the old lady because she was so ill and was in need of constant attention. The first things she noticed were small beams of light which seemed to come from one corner of the room and make their way round the walls. One night there seemed to be more lights than usual and she asked her aunt what she thought they were, but her aunt could see nothing, yet all the while they hovered over the sick woman.

The following evening her aunt fell asleep earlier than usual, but Mrs Brittlebank remained awake. It was in the early hours of the morning that she was disturbed by a noise outside the bedroom door. The latch was being lifted and into the room walked two figures. Mrs Brittlebank sat up in bed terrified, unable to do anything, her limbs frozen. All she could do was to watch. As suddenly as they appeared they vanished. It must be noted that this happened at a time when a small paraffin lamp was burning in the room, so the place was not in complete darkness. Who were these figures – the precursors of death? It was not long after that her aunt died.

Following this, every morning between six and seven o'clock, a noise could be heard, as though someone was unrolling paper and cutting it. The lights began to go on and off. The living-room light would be switched off and the one in the kitchen would be switched on. Footsteps could be heard frequently walking about the house and a strange whistling noise. When the footsteps trod the stairs they were heavy as though a man was stamping up the stairs in heavy boots.

Crockery, pans and other domestic utensils began to move, or rather were thrown about. Pans would come off shelves and fall to the floor with a tremendous clatter. The growling of a dog could be heard coming from the hearth, although nothing was actually seen except on the one occasion previously mentioned. Knocks at the door were frequent, but always, when opened, there was no one there.

On one occasion Mrs Brittlebank had her cardigan torn from off her back. The bedclothes were violently thrown on to the floor, curtains would fall down from the windows, and often there was the feeling that something cold was passing, like a gust of wind.

Exorcisms have been held in the cottage, but not one has been successful, in fact Mrs Brittlebank believes that the happenings became more frequent and much worse. It was as though there was a tremendous battle taking place between the forces of good and evil.

Eventually, both Mr Wood and Mrs Brittlebank had to leave the cottage. They felt that the house was not only haunted, but that there was something dreadfully evil in the place, as though they were being driven out. Mrs Brittlebank's nerves suffered very badly because of these experiences. Of course she knows that many people believe that they were hallucinations, the result of an overworked imagination, but there are the testimonies of others to consider.

What evil influence is there in that cottage? What terrible deed was committed, perhaps centuries ago? The answers will never be known, but whatever the history of the place it seems quite certain that evil is abroad in that cottage.

Staffordshire

The White Rabbit

The appearance of phantom animals is sometimes thought to predict death either to the person who sees the spirit or to someone closely connected with him. The animal might take any form, a dog, a cat, a rabbit or practically any kind of domestic pet. The late Elliott O'Donnell has written a number of accounts in which phantom animals have figured prominently. He records how a black cat was seen at a large house in Oxenby, but its appearance used to strike terror into the hearts of those who saw the beast, for it uttered the most piteous cries and seemed to be in a death-agony.

One has only to make reference to the haunting of Checkley Rectory, mentioned in this book, to learn that the ghost of Mrs Hutchinson was usually accompanied by a phantom dog. Sometimes the animal was seen by itself in the rectory.

The two stories which follow are about a phantom white rabbit, but it might be that both accounts are one and the same although they were supposedly seen in two different places, miles apart.

The first story takes us back to the middle of the last century. In those days there was no direct road from Etruria to Hanley, only a bye-path across the fields. The way from Etruria to Cobridge was a very lonely route made eerie by trees on each side of the path hanging over and intertwining to form a complete canopy. At night strange noises were heard; the piercing voice of a boy in great distress, of a boy who desperately screamed for help. The voice would stop as suddenly as it had begun and all would be deathly still. Then there would appear the form of a milk-white rabbit. It would jump out from one side of the road and run along the path for a short distance and then just disappear. It is said that it always took the same route.

The place where this used to happen was called The Grove

and the local people regarded it as a place to be avoided. Any midnight rake having made merry in Hanley and returning by way of The Grove was usually sober by the time he reached that dreadful spot.

Apparently one man made up his mind to see if he could catch this rabbit about which he had heard so much. Night after night he bravely kept his lonely vigil until one dark evening his waiting was rewarded. Sure enough there came the awful screams crying out for mercy, and then silence. A few moments later there appeared a white rabbit coming down the path straight towards the man. When the animal was immediately opposite him he pounced and was quite certain that he had caught it, but there was nothing there. His hands had passed right through the creature and he received a dislocated shoulder for his trouble.

The story behind this particular haunting is a gruesome one. Near to where the rabbit was seen was Crabtree Field, which was bordered by trees four or five deep. Sloping from the trees was a narrow dell, through which ran a stream carried under the canal by means of a culvert. At the bottom of the dell was a thick hedgerow. The deep ditch through which the stream ran was thickly covered with brambles; the whole aspect of the area in the daytime was one of great natural beauty.

Next to the field was what was locally known as the prison-bar field which was given by Josiah Wedgwood for a playground. The field was separated from the canal by a thick hawthorn hedge.

One Saturday afternoon in August 1833 two boys, one aged sixteen, the other fourteen, were making their way along the canal bank towards Burslem. They stopped and crawled through the hedge and entered Crabtree Field. For hours they played the game of 'pitch and toss'. As darkness came on they had difficulty in seeing whether the coin fell heads or tails uppermost. The older boy had lost nearly all his money, which happened to be his wages for the week. He quarrelled violently with the younger one and was in such a rage that he grasped the boy by the throat and squeezed the last breath out of him, all the time ignoring his piteous cries for help and mercy.

The older boy looked at his lifeless victim. He picked up all the money and then began the work of disposing of the body. He was well aware what the punishment for such a ghastly crime would be, so he endeavoured to make the death look like suicide. He dragged the corpse into the dell and there hung the body from the branch of one of the trees.

It was some time before it was discovered by some of the villagers and one can imagine their horror at finding this partly decomposed body suspended by the neck.

Eventually the youth who had committed the crime was arrested, tried and sentenced to death, but because of his age the sentence was commuted to transportation for life. There are records to prove that this crime was actually committed. The name of the murderer was Charles Shaw and the victim John Holdcroft, both boys were from Burslem and they had often been seen together. Shaw was tried for the murder in March 1834.

There is a story of another white rabbit which was seen by a number of people in the Kidsgrove area. Occasionally the creature crossed the avenue leading to Clough Hall and its appearance was said to be a prediction of death. One person who saw the animal said that three days after the incident his father died. Others too have spoken of seeing the rabbit and people who have been related, or who have been close friends, have died.

Today such an incident would be regarded as superstition, a story fabricated to arouse local interest, but in those days people tended to believe that such happenings often had ominous meanings. The stories of the phantom rabbits may or may not be true, but they were to the largely superstitious inhabitants at that time.

Hatherton Hall

Approximately one mile due west of Cannock in Staffordshire and in a lovely part of Cannock Chase stands Hatherton Hall. Its isolated position suggests it as a suitable spot for a haunting and, indeed, the Hall has the reputation of having two ghosts; or are they one and the same?

One Christmas Eve in the middle of the nineteenth century a party of men met at Hatherton Hall for the seasonal festivities. The ladies were at a ball and the men were waiting for their return. The drink was flowing freely and in a short time there was none left. Lord Hatherton ordered the butler to bring up some bottles of the family port from the cellar where it had been kept for over twenty years. When the rare vintage was eventually brought up his Lordship and his guests retired to the study. There they examined guns, swords, foxes' brushes and stags' heads which adorned the walls of the spacious and beautifully furnished room.

One of the guests noticed an unusual object on the desk – unusual because it was shaped in the form of a human skull. He picked it up and to his horror discovered that what he held in his hands was no imitation but the real thing. He quickly replaced it and found some difficulty in hiding his revulsion. Lord Hatherton had noticed his guest's action and subsequent discomfort and walked over to the desk and calmly picked up the skull so that everyone could see it.

Lord Hatherton was asked about it and explained that it was now a drinking vessel, but had indeed been the head of one of his most illustrious ancestors, Sir Hugh de Hatherton.

Some years ago the skeleton of Sir Hugh was dug up where a private chapel once stood and the skull was separated from the rest of the body, lined with silver and used as a drinking cup. Many of the guests felt that there was something macabre about the object and that its use was a form of desecration, but they were filled with wine and any fears that they might have had were soon forgotten.

The skull was there and then filled with Burgundy and every man drank from it, all declaring that wine had never tasted so good. Such was the merriment of the guests that they even drank the health of the departed lord of the manor. They even asked for his presence among them so that he could share in the celebration, and Lord Hatherton said that he would surrender the skull should Sir Hugh appear. Little did they realise that their macabre joke was to have a ghastly and terrifying result.

At the last stroke of twelve the goblet was placed on the desk, and suddenly footfalls were heard in the long corridor which led to the study. Someone suggested that the ladies had returned from the ball. But the sound was that of only one person, and the tread was heavy like that of a man. A late guest perhaps? But all who had been invited had arrived; no guest was missing. Then to the horror of those in the study the skull began to move. It rolled very slowly across the desk and fell to the floor, and appeared to roll underneath the desk.

Suddenly the door of the study opened and there in the open doorway stood the headless form of a knight in armour. It made no noise. The limbs of the guests were rendered useless – they froze with the horror which the spectre evoked. The figure bowed and then turned, and the noise of the receding footsteps could be heard retreating along the corridor.

The arrival of the ladies from the ball helped to relieve the tense atmosphere. The following morning an intensive search of the study and the rest of the hall was made, but the skull was nowhere to be found.

Lord Hatherton's study opened on to a large lawn and it was here that one of the guests saw a silver object on the grass. It was found to be the thin silver plate which had lined the skull goblet. The skull itself was never found. Sir Hugh de Hatherton had come to claim what was rightly his, no doubt disturbed and insulted by the frivolous use to which his skull had been put.

The second story is of another haunting at Hatherton Hall and involves the well known ghost-hunters, the late Elliott O'Donnell and Mr Byford-Jones. Lord and Lady Hatherton invited them to investigate a number of curious happenings thought to be connected with the apparition of a tall man in a cloak who had been seen in one of the rooms.

O'Donnell and Byford-Jones were met by Lord Hatherton – his wife had been unexpectedly called away – and his two daughters, the Hon. Mrs Gardner and the Hon. Hester Littleton. The visitors were told the full story of the ghost.

What might have been the sound of footsteps was heard on the stairs at night but little attention was paid to them as stairs in old houses often creak. A woman who slept in a bedroom in the old part of the house (parts date from 1613) said that she had seen the ghost of a tall man in a cloak. Later, two other people saw the ghost and other manifestations but neither was aware that the Hall was reputed to be haunted.

The real reason why O'Donnell and Byford-Jones had been asked to the Hall was because the gardener had had a terrible experience which had left him unwell for some time. The details of this experience, at the gardener's request, may not be related, but he had been very badly shaken.

The ghost was said not to appear to members of the family, but Mrs Gardner once had an uncanny experience. One night she was awakened by a heavy breathing noise in a part of her bedroom. It seemed to be the noise of an animal and, on hearing it, a dog which always slept in her bedroom began to whine pitifully. The breathing seemed to go right round the room and then stopped. The rest of the family were roused and a thorough search made, but nothing was discovered. Later that night the sound began again and this time the dog showed signs of great terror.

After dinner, O'Donnell, Byford-Jones, the two ladies and a fifth member of the party his name is not given – agreed to keep vigil in the bedroom where the noise had been heard. It was nearly eleven o'clock when they went to the haunted room, where they sat in the firelight until two o'clock with visits to three other rooms during that time.

The coal fire burned fitfully and there were intervals of darkness. Everyone remained quiet. Suddenly a white figure loomed out of the gloom, came straight towards them and then disappeared.

One of the party declared that there were noises outside the room and then inside, as if someone were knocking. Mr X, the unnamed guest, became very uneasy. O'Donnell had the feeling that someone or something was moving about the house; he heard the opening and shutting of a door. O'Donnell and Mr X later visited the room where the figure in the cloak had been seen. The silence in the house was by this time most oppressive. They had been in the room only a short time when Mr X said that he was convinced that he could hear sounds and he pointed to some curtains by the window. O'Donnell was quite certain that the curtains moved mysteriously. Mr X felt that he could no longer remain in the room, but as they were about to leave they were joined by Byford-Jones and Lord Hatherton's two daughters and all three said that they had heard nothing during the half-hour they had spent together.

Suddenly Mr X flashed his torch and in a trembling voice said that he could hear the sounds of heavy breathing. He felt something near him which touched his elbow and made him feel icy cold and distinctly ill.

Nothing else was heard or felt and certainly nothing had been seen, except the white figure.

Margaret Leigh

Margaret Leigh was born in Burslem about 1685. The exact date of her birth is not known although the date of her death is; and there was good reason to remember her death, for ensuing events were to strike terror into the minds of many who believed that they had seen her wandering about the streets years after her burial.

Burslem was then a small pottery village surrounded by forest and woodland, very different from what it is today, where as the centre of the pottery industry, row upon row of terraced houses stand where once trees and flowers flourished.

Margaret Leigh was born into a family which was well respected and highly esteemed in that part of the North Midlands. Incidentally, the surname is sometimes spelt Lee, but my researches have made it quite clear that the former spelling is the correct one. Her home was a farm, probably early Elizabethan, and although the building itself was not large it was situated in extensive grounds.

It seems that Margaret Leigh was an ugly child and somewhat malformed. Little is known of her childhood, but when she was older she moved away from her birthplace and lived in a small isolated cottage. It is said that she was turned out of her home by the rest of her family and this was the beginning of a time of real hardship for this unfortunate woman, whose life was made intolerable by the villagers, and especially by the parson who saw to it that she should be regarded as the local witch.

She managed to earn a meagre living by keeping a few cows and selling milk, but it was not long before whispers began to get about that she sold short measure and even diluted the milk with water. It appears that she was a very enterprising person and a woman of some business acumen, for she established a savings bank! It is reported that those who invested their money never received any interest. Perhaps they were too afraid to resist her requests for deposits and too terrified to question what use was made of it.

The so-called witch of Burslem was said to have the 'evil eye' – no doubt a reference to an exaggerated squint which added to her ugly appearance. It was said that wherever she went a blackbird could be seen sitting on her shoulder; this would be regarded as her 'familiar', the symbol of evil, and therefore showed she was in league with the Devil.

The local parson figures prominently in this story and from all accounts he was a notoriously uncharitable man who could drink most people under the table at the local hostelry. The Rev. Spencer was rector of the old church at Burslem but he appears to have taken more interest in his liquor than in his parishioners. He crossed Margaret Leigh's path because she refused to attend church and, probably out of spite, he denounced her as a witch. Just how seriously this was taken is difficult to ascertain because witchcraft was considered a very serious crime, yet she escaped being convicted and it seems that she was never the victim of any witch-hunt.

In April 1748 Margaret Leigh died. The burial took place on a cold and dismal day and Parson Spencer no doubt used the inclement weather as justification for a visit to the Turk's Head immediately after the interment. It was in this place that previously he had proclaimed that Margaret Leigh was in communion with the Devil and therefore a witch.

After he had been in the Turk's Head, Parson Spencer suggested that he and some others should visit the dead woman's cottage. On arrival Spencer walked boldly to the door, pushed it open and went in, the rest staying at a safe distance some way from the door. Suddenly there came a howl from inside the cottage and Parson Spencer came rushing out as though the Devil himself was in pursuit. He spoke to no one as he fled past the others in the direction of the Turk's Head, his face contorted with terror.

The others, not knowing what had happened, followed after him but it was some time before Spencer was in a fit state to relate his ghastly experience. At last, calmed by much ale, he told the wide-eyed listeners that when he opened the cottage door he walked straight into the room and to his surprise found a fire burning in the fireplace although no one had been in the cottage for days. He then experienced a feeling of what can only be described as sheer terror. His body went ice cold and his eyes were drawn to the corner of the room where, to his horror, he saw the woman whom he had only a few hours ago buried, sitting on her stool and looking at him with an evil smile on her face. It was a look of triumph.

From that time many people claimed to have seen her walking the streets of the village and although few liked her when she was alive, all were terrified of her when she was dead. It was said that as she walked the streets she could be heard to say:

'Weight and measure sold I never,
Milk and water sold I ever.'

People became so terrified that none dare to go out at night and the villagers pleaded with Parson Spencer to do something to rid them of the terror by night. At length he agreed and procured the help of three other clergymen from Wolstanton, Newchapel and Stoke. With the additional help of Spencer's sexton and clerk they went to the churchyard at dead of night and resolved to dig up the coffin and exorcise the earthbound soul. They had been digging for some minutes when it was felt that they were all being watched by some malignant presence. The atmosphere proved too much for Parson Spencer's three companions and they quickly left. With his sexton and clerk Spencer continued to dig until they reached the coffin. By this time Spencer was shaking with uncontrolled terror and his sexton and clerk were in no better condition. Now came the worst part of the work – that of opening the coffin. At last the lid was removed, and a live blackbird was placed beside the body and the lid of the coffin quickly refastened. But the work was not yet over. Spencer decided that to make absolutely certain there should be no more appearances of the apparition the coffin should be turned at right angles to its original position. So the grave was widened and the coffin turned. The work completed, they returned to their homes. The parson drank away his feelings of horror and revulsion.

The news spread in the village – at last she was gone; but there was not one person who would go near the graveyard at night. There is a rhyme which, if said while running around the grave three times, is supposed to raise the ghostly form again.

'Molly Leigh, follow me
Around all the graves you can see.'

There are a number of variations of the story and it is not surprising after a period of about three hundred years. According to one story the ghost of Margaret Leigh used to appear in the houses of people and sit knitting in a corner of a room.

One account of the laying of her ghost described how six clergymen brought a stone pig-trough and, placing it in the middle of the church, they prayed for hours that her spirit might find rest. Eventually they saw her hovering above them and as they continued to pray the form was slowly drawn down towards them, face downwards. At last they got her into the trough and buried her in the churchyard.

There is a very similar story of an unscrupulous milkmaid who lived in the centre of Shrewsbury. It is said that because of her dishonesty her soul could find no peace and she was destined to wander, constantly compelled to repeat the words:

'Weight and measure sold I never,
Milk and water sold I ever.'

These two stories might be one and the same, or they may have become confused. Today, the grave of Margaret Leigh can be seen in St John's churchyard, Burslem, and the headstone is the only one in a transverse position to the rest.

I think this is one of the most interesting tales I have heard, but no doubt much has been added to what is actual fact. Our forefathers were superstitious and they feared the dead, believing that a person's influence was stronger after death, but it was strongly believed that the Church had its part to play in the work of finding a resting place for the restless souls of the departed. Today the clergy are not infrequently called upon to conduct an exorcism – but, I hope, not in the manner of Parson Spencer. I feel that considerable Dutch courage would be needed to tackle the job in such a way.

Staffordshire

The Man-Eating Family of the Moors

If any reader has visited the remote regions of North Staffordshire, you cannot fail to be impressed by the sheer vastness of the moors. They are wild, and dangerous when the weather shows its inclement face. The Roches, an outcrop of dark, forbidding rock, weirdly shaped and serrating the skyline, is a rock-climber's paradise.

There is a unique beauty about the place. The very grandeur of the rocks gives one a sense of primeval purity. Here have stood these ancient sentinels for hundreds of thousands of years and today they command Man's respect. Modernity has not touched or defiled them. They remain a reminder of Man's transitoriness.

From October to March the moorland presents an unrivalled picture of bleakness – the sheer vastness of it makes one feel microscopic. It can be beautiful, but it can be savage. When the wind and the rain sweep over these coarse grassed hills the face of nature can be cruel.

It is little wonder that stories of strange people, terrible murders and fearful happenings are part of its history.

The story is told of a pedlar who, very many years ago, was lost on this stretch of moorland. Where he came from or where he was going no one seems to know, but in those days men and women used to walk the lonely moorland tracks calling at the towns and villages selling whatever they had.

The weather was foul and night was drawing in sharply like a dark shroud. The pedlar thought that he might have to spend the night out of doors; a dismal prospect. In the distance he saw a light, faint at first, but as he approached it became brighter. To his joy it was the oil lamp of some cottage, a cheering light on such a night. Surely he would be given shelter, if only until the storm abated.

He knocked on the door, but there was no reply. A further and louder knock brought someone to the door. Bolts were drawn back and the door opened. There standing in the doorway was a young boy. The pedlar asked if he might shelter for a while. The boy made no reply but looked him up and down and invited him into the cottage.

When he was inside he was made comfortable by the fire and he began to speak about his journey and how he had lost his way. There was an uncanny silence in the cottage. The family spoke very little, but they looked at him with an intensity that made the pedlar's blood run cold.

The boy who had opened the door to let the pedlar into the cottage came alongside him and began to touch the man's hands and feel his face. He heard the words, 'What nice pies the hands would make!' To his horror the pedlar realised that he was in the cottage of a family who were reputed to eat people. He had heard the story from some of the moorland folk and this night, in his blindness, he had walked right into their house.

But his terror did not leave him immobilised. He got out of his chair and made for the door. His fear gave him such determination that somehow he managed to beat off the monsters and get outside the cottage.

On he ran, running into the teeth of the storm, but with one thought in mind, to escape from that house of horrors. Behind him were his unnatural pursuers. He came to a river and without considering the consequences jumped in. He blindly groped for the bank and finally hid himself under the overhanging roots of a tree. He remained up to his neck in the cold water until the fiends gave up their search.

As soon as he was certain they had left he climbed out of the water and made for the nearest town. It is said that he brought the officers of justice to the cottage and the family were arrested and subsequently hanged, the house being razed to the ground.

There are no records of such a trial taking place, but people long afterwards were convinced that they could hear the noise of the ghastly chase. The unearthly shouts of the ghoulish family could be heard above the roar of a storm and few would venture out on such a night.

Staffordshire

The Walking Dead

Many castles and mansions are reputed to be haunted by some former occupant who met with a tragic end. Some stories no doubt are true, having been well authenticated on a number of occasions, whilst others are completely fictitious. But these places do have atmospheres and with long passages, oak-panelled rooms and the like it is not surprising that they 'acquire' a ghost. The rest is left to imagination, which in some instances needs little encouragement.

It has been my experience to discover that where there is almost definite proof of a haunting there is a certain amount of reticence displayed by the people concerned. I am suspicious when I am subjected to loquacious descriptions of an experience 'definitely' supernatural – few people who have come into contact with what they feel is the supernatural care to advertise this. Of course there are reasons for such a reluctance to impart this kind of information. For one thing, they may feel that they will leave themselves open to ridicule and, secondly, it may attract a lot of inquisitive people who have little respect for other people's privacy. There is the feeling of scepticism to take into account. I have spoken to numerous people who have told me about unusual happenings and the first thing they have done is to try to rationalise their experience, trying hard to convince themselves that there must be some kind of scientific explanation. I have met others who firmly believe right from the beginning that their experience was that of the supernatural. They might be correct in their conclusions, but I am careful not to accept as evidence of the supernatural everything that is said, especially if I detect a considerable enthusiasm displayed in relating the facts. However, the latter have been a very small minority and it has taken time, patience and a good deal of work to extract the right kind of material. I am more likely to be convinced that a place is haunted when the person or persons concerned are themselves uncertain, and not given to over-enthusiasm in disclosing information.

The following story leaves me in no doubt that here was an incursion into the realms of the supernatural.

Six miles north of Uttoxeter and the same distance south-west of Ashbourne stands Alton Towers, former home of the Earls of Shrewsbury. It stands on a thickly wooded hill overlooking the beautiful Churnet Valley. The Talbots, which is the name of the Earls of Shrewsbury go back a long time in history, but the site of Alton Towers goes back farther still, for the hill on which the mansion is built is probably the site of an Iron Age camp.

Today the grounds are open to the public and there are numerous facilities for children's recreation. The grounds are very extensive, offering delightful picnic areas, and visitors come in their thousands. There is a great Rock Garden with Japanese maples and dwarf conifers on the steep and naturally rocky slopes. Fountains, bridges, and ornamental gardens can be seen in abundance.

It was in December 1969 that I visited the foreman of the Alton Towers estate. I remember it very distinctly for the day was dreary, the rain falling heavily and the mist hanging over the Churnet Valley like a shroud. In the comfortable warmth of the estate lodge Mr Noakes told me about something which he had seen nearly forty years ago. I was very impressed with his story. He was a man unafraid of the dark. His job involved walking round the gardens at all hours and there are some places in the grounds that take on an eerie atmosphere as darkness approaches. He is a very level-headed person, practical and certainly not given to imagining things.

The experience took place before he was married and he had just seen his fiancée, now Mrs Noakes, on to the train. On the southern side of the Towers was a railway station, now disused, and the track ran parallel with the river Churnet for quite some distance. Today the route can still be seen, but there are no rails. The way back to the lodge was by way of the 'Step Walk'. This path winds upwards through a heavily wooded part of the grounds and has no less than eighteen flights of steps, each flight consisting of about twelve steps.

The time was approximately nine forty-five in the evening as Mr Noakes made his way back along his favourite route. He had walked that same path scores of times both at night as well as in the day. Between each flight of steps there is a distance of about fifty yards and it was when he was approaching the last flight of steps that he saw someone standing right at the very top.

Mr Noakes thought that he would be about thirty yards or so from the spot where the figure stood, but he took little notice, thinking that it was someone who was visiting the house and was taking a stroll in the grounds. Certainly the thought of a ghost never entered his head. As Mr Noakes approached the steps the figure began to descend.

Mr Noakes noticed his mode of dress and could not help seeing how bright his shoes shone, as though they were patent leather. He was wearing a tall dark hat and a long flowing black cape. A white silk scarf hung loosely from his shoulders and in one hand he carried what appeared to be a silver-topped black ebony walking cane.

As the figure drew level with Mr Noakes the latter said, 'Good evening'. As soon as he uttered the words the man vanished. Mr Noakes stopped dead in his tracks. He looked for the person to whom he had spoken – but there was no one there. To his left was a large overhanging rock, to his right a steep grassy slope. The moon shone very brightly, offering considerable light to see for some distance in every direction. No amount of searching revealed the whereabouts of the person. Mr Noakes ran home as fast as he could. The hair on the back of his neck prickled and an icy feeling crept down his spine.

When he arrived home he told his father about the figure he had seen, but it was viewed with some scepticism.

The following day while the gardeners were having their mid-morning break Mr Noakes told his story to some of his workmates. Again the reaction was one of lightly passing it off as imagination. But there was one man, older than the others, who had worked on the estate many years, who did not scorn what he had heard. He asked Mr Noakes if he had seen a black dog accompanying the figure. Mr Noakes said that he had not seen such a dog. The older man said that he had seen the figure on a number of occasions but each time there had been a black dog with it. He also knew about an accident that had happened many years ago at the place where the figure had been seen.

It appears that there had been a party given at Farley Hall, a large house not far distant from Alton Towers, and a guest walked from there to the Towers, presumably where he was being accommodated. The following morning his dead body was found at the top of the last flight of steps on the 'Step Walk'. The reason for his death is unknown, but murder can certainly be ruled out. It is more likely that he suffered a heart attack and collapsed and died, but even this must be regarded as conjecture.

Shortly afterwards, Mr Noakes' father saw the figure and this time there was a black dog with it. The spectre has been seen very infrequently and only once by Mr Noakes. Who is the man in black? What was he doing at the top of the 'Step Walk', for he was going away from the house? Will the riddle ever be solved? I wonder if he walks today.

Throwley Hall

There are numerous stories concerning phantom horses, headless horsemen, ghostly dogs and the like, which haunt the roads and country lanes of every county. Staffordshire is not without its share of phantom coaches and horses, and the story which follows will, I hope, make you have second thoughts about dismissing such things as fanciful imagination.

I have gone to a great deal of trouble to ensure that the facts stated are true, and from my investigations I feel that there is a ring of authenticity about this particular manifestation, for I have spoken to and corresponded with quite a number of independent witnesses and each account of his or her particular experience reveals a startling similarity of detail when comparisons are made.

But first of all let us find out just how the story began. What is the history behind the phantom coach and horses which are often heard but never seen near Throwley Hall?

Deep in the beautiful and winding Manifold Valley stands the ruins of Throwley Hall, one-time residence of the Cromwell family. Today there is little left of the place, not even the shell of the building remains, just a couple of walls, the rest a heap of stone and rubble. But there is an atmosphere about the place, an atmosphere which is difficult to describe. One has the feeling of foreboding as though the place has some ghastly crime to hide, and, as I later discovered, it has.

During the time of Cromwell some members of the family went to Ashbourne in the family coach, a distance of approximately six miles, the coachman returning to the Hall after he had left them at their destination, with orders to return and collect them in the evening. At about midday a torrential storm unleashed itself and the valley was shrouded in thick cloud whilst the road from the Hall became a quagmire. The coachman very reluctantly, but under orders, set off for Ashbourne to bring back the rest of the family. The horses slithered in the mud and the coach lurched violently from side to side. Eventually the steaming team arrived at Ashbourne and the return journey began.

The narrow road twisted snake-like through the valley and in places ran closely parallel to the river Manifold. The torrential rain, descending like an unbroken sheet of water, had swollen the river to a dangerous height. The storm worsened in its severity. Lightning lit up the sky for miles around and the deafening crash of thunder added to the nightmare of the journey. On more than one occasion the men in the coach were obliged to get out and help the coachman when the carriage wheels stuck in the mud. Sweat poured off the terrified horses. Suddenly there came a flash of lightning more brilliant than any before, followed by a crash of thunder as though the heavens had been torn apart by some angry god. This was too much for the horses. With screams of terror they fled along the treacherous ground, the coachman losing control. The fear that had gripped the creatures drove them forward, but blinded them to direction. The close proximity of the river brought this awful drama to a conclusion. Horses, coach and occupants were flung into the swollen water and, needless to say, all were drowned.

The tragedy brought considerable grief to the Cromwell family and ever since that dreadful night it is said that the hoof-beats of the phantom horses can be heard thundering along the road which leads to the Hall.

Today there is a narrow winding road leading through the valley, and part of this was the original drive to the Hall; it is along a particular stretch of this road that the phantom hoof-beats have been heard by quite a number of people.

A Mrs Phillips wrote to me in a letter dated 6th October 1969, telling me of her experience. She was sixteen at the time and was walking along the road previously mentioned. At that time she lived in the village of Ilam, which is about three miles from Throwley Hall. As she made her way along the road she suddenly heard the sound of galloping horses coming from behind. The noise grew louder and she distinctly heard the noise of wheels, as though a cart was being pulled at a tremendous speed. She quickly moved to one side and stepped off the road, thinking that whatever was approaching had better have as much road as possible. To her horror she saw nothing. The noise came nearer until it was almost deafening. There was the noise of heavy breathing as though horses were being driven beyond their capacity. The thundering roar of horses' hooves and the rattle of wheels went past her. She stood frozen to the spot – she had often heard of the legend, but this was the first and only time she had experienced it.

In 1963 Mrs Phillips wrote to a local newspaper in answer to a request for local legends and related her experience. Within a few days she received a letter from someone in Ashbourne who claimed that her husband had heard the same terrifying noise in almost the same place – and in broad daylight, but there was nothing to be seen. I have also seen other correspondence written over a period of twenty years by independent witnesses, who lay claim to having heard the phantom hoofbeats.

Now it so happened that in late October 1969 I was to lead a conference of young people from Congregational Churches in North Staffordshire, so I took the opportunity of visiting Throwley Hall. I must say that I did not hear anything resembling horses' hoofbeats, but I did speak to the local farmer who had one or two very interesting things to tell me.

Between the ruins of the Hall and a large building of the same period stands a farmhouse of more recent date. In conversation with the farmer I gleaned bits of information about the history of the Hall and then I asked him about the legend of the phantom horses. He looked me straight in the eye and said, 'You want to know about that, do you? Well, I can tell you that it's true.'

I told him what I had heard and the information I had received from different people. He continued, 'What they have told you is true. I've often heard them. Why, only a few nights ago, whilst I was watching television, I heard them come right into the yard. Shod horses they were, and judging from the noise they made they were in a 'ell of a sweat.'

I asked him if he knew for sure if they were the phantom horses. He replied, 'Of course they were – you see, there was nothing to be seen and we haven't got an 'orse on the farm.'

There are no doubts whatever in this farmer's mind that the phantom horses exist – he has heard them too often. I thought that I had come to the end of the conversation when he mentioned something else of interest.

'You know,' he said, 'Cromwell wasn't a man to be played with; if anyone opened their mouth and what they said got his back up, their heads would roll – and it happened here too.'

I questioned him further about this. He couldn't recall exact details, but he told me that a lady who was at the Hall gravely displeased the fanatical Puritan, and for her audacity she was beheaded.

He went on, 'It was about three or four months ago. It was a grand night, the moon shone brilliantly. I was leaning on the wall' (he indicated this with his finger) 'looking at the old Hall when the hairs on the back of my neck began to prickle. I was rooted to the spot, but I couldn't take my eyes off what I saw. Standing in what had been a doorway in the Hall was the figure of a headless woman. She didn't move, she just stood there. She was dressed in white and down the front of the long dress was a dark patch, I don't know what it was, I couldn't make it out, but I suppose it could have been blood. I can tell you I was terrified – but I couldn't take my eyes off her, then she just went. I've never seen her since and I don't want to, either.'

So the phantom horses still pull the carriage with its ghostly occupants and the headless lady still appears as evidence of the brutality she suffered.

Witches

Until the end of the eighteenth century it was firmly believed that witches existed, men and women who had sold their souls to the Devil and who practised such wickedness as to bring all manner of evil to people when they cast their spells. Even after the eighteenth century the belief in witches was not entirely dead. In many country districts, superstitions still lingered and many an old woman was tormented by the taunts of frightened villagers. During the sixteenth and seventeenth centuries witchcraft and the persecution of people suspected of witchcraft prevailed. Church and government in turn hunted out witches, many of whom were executed in a most barbaric manner on the flimsiest and often most ridiculous evidence.

Confessions, so called, were extracted from suspects and the practice of looking for certain marks on the human body which were supposed to indicate the person to be a witch, was in itself revolting. A person could bring a charge of witchcraft against someone he did not like, and if he lost any of his animal stock or there was illness in the family, it wasn't a difficult task to concoct stories of spells being cast. Many of the witch trials subjected men and women to unbelievable bestiality and it was not uncommon for people to take the law into their own hands and institute witch-hunts, the poor unfortunate person suffering the most agonising abuses, until death brought them a happy release. All this may seem to us in the twentieth century somewhat uncivilised, but we must remember that the sixteenth and seventeenth centuries were a period of superstition and that the Church thought that it was doing the right thing in persecuting these people. After all, they believed them to be in league with the Devil, the arch-enemy of Almighty God!

Many books have been written about witchcraft in this country and abroad and there is an abundance of information which is historically interesting for the student who wishes to pursue the subject. My sympathy is with the witches themselves. They were subjected to the worst forms of degradation and indignities.

It was believed that witches could change themselves into animals, a belief which was very firmly held. In this country it was believed that witches had the power to turn themselves into an animal so that they could make good their escape from those who hunted them or because in the disguise of an animal it was easier to rob a farmer of his stock. People believe that witches could turn themselves into any animal they wished, but the commonest one was the hare, probably because it was an animal difficult to capture on account of its tremendous speed over the roughest terrain.

A story is told of a woman who lived near Leek in North Staffordshire. She was suspected of being a witch and was subjected to much gossip. The poor woman knew no peace. One day some men were out hunting and they saw a hare sitting in the middle of a field. They gave chase and on this occasion the animal was nearly caught. The dogs kept up with the horses and one dog in particular forged ahead of the rest of the party and as the hare jumped over a wall the dog was able to snap at the animal and managed to bite out some of the fur. However, the wall was too high for the dog to get over, and there the chase ended. One of the huntsmen who had seen the near miss rode up to the wall thinking that perhaps the hare might still be in sight and possibly wounded. He dismounted, climbed the wall, and there on the other side, squatting on her haunches, was an old woman rubbing her head from which there was a substantial amount of hair missing. So runs the story, but perhaps the huntsman had previously alienated himself from the woman and made up the story to really convince others that this person was definitely a witch!

My second story concerns a visit I made to a farm at Little Onn, not far from Stafford. Mr Norman White, who owns nearly four hundred acres, gladly took me to the place where a witch was supposed to have milked a cow before going on to Nottingham. We went across the farmyard and stood outside a small dark outbuilding. According to his father and his grandfather, it was in this very place that the witch was seen milking one of the cows, but the strange thing about it was that she was milking into a sieve! One wit to whom I told the story suggested that perhaps she was the first person to make separated milk.

I asked Mr White how long ago this was, but he had no idea. The story had been handed down through the family for generations.

He then showed me a stone or rather a small boulder which was to the side of the farmyard. There was supposed to be the print of a cow's hoof on the surface. On inspection there could be seen a perfect imprint of a cow's hoof, the shape and size fitting exactly. How it came to be there he did not know, but it had something to do with the witch, and the legend was that if anyone moved the stone then disaster would befall the farm. I asked him if he really believed this and he said that he didn't, but when I asked him if he was prepared to move the stone to test out the story he refused; the stone would stay where it had always been. Are we yet rid of our superstitions? I don't think so.

Close to the farm in one of the fields is a very old well. Many years ago some nuns wanted to build a church there because they regarded the water as being holy. Mr White told me that the level of the water in the well never alters whether there is a lot of rain or a long dry spell. Was it because of this that the nuns believed the water to be holy? It is a known fact that babies were baptised with the water from the well. They did not get their wishes granted, for the church was eventually built in a village a few miles distant. Of course, this story has nothing to do with witches, but I found it very interesting and as it was on the same farm where the witch was supposed to have been I thought it worth recording.

A Dog's Terror

In reply to a request for strange stories and hauntings which was published in the *Walsall Observer* on 28th November 1969, a Miss A. L. Burnell wrote to me about an incident concerning the alarming behaviour of her dog.

We have to go back to the years of the Second World War when Miss Burnell was taking a holiday with her father in the Quinton area of Worcestershire. They were strangers to the place, but being very fond of the countryside they took every opportunity to explore their new and beautiful surroundings. When they went walking they always took their dog, Paddy, with them. As Miss Burnell and her father were not familiar with this part of Worcestershire, many of the well known beauty spots were not known to them at the time.

Eventually they came to what they later learned was Hagley Wood and it was here that the dog behaved in a most unusual manner. To quote Miss Burnell. '. . . the dog went completely berserk and fled along the road terrified. I ran along after him and managed to catch him. I picked him up and he was shaking and moaning. We continued our walk and of course not knowing our way around we had to return by the same route. Exactly the same thing happened to the dog in exactly the same place. Later on in the week we took the same walk again and of course the inevitable happened, except that this time when I caught up with the dog he flung himself into my arms shaking with sheer terror and digging his claws into my shoulders. Sometime afterwards we read in the *Sunday Mercury* that a skeleton had been found in a hollow tree in Hagley Wood. Incidentally, my dog never showed any signs of terror before or after this occasion.'

I wrote a second letter to Miss Burnell asking her to give me a definite date if it were possible. In her reply she said that it was a long time ago and she could not remember the exact date, but she knew that in the area there were some prisoners of war working on some of the local farms. Not far away, at Long Marston, there was a war prisoners' camp which held mainlv German, Italian and Ukrainian prisoners.

Before we begin to ask why her dog behaved in such a strange way we must look at some facts concerning the discovery of the skeleton in an old wych elm in Hagley Wood and the subsequent discovery that a crime so horrible had been committed as to be both macabre and sinister. The following details are based on chapter four in the book by Donald McCormick, *Murder by Witchcraft*, published in 1968. I am most grateful to Mr McCormick for his permission to use his material this way.

It was on a Sunday evening in April 1943 that three boys went birdnesting in Hagley Wood. The boys were Robert Hart and Thomas Willets, both aged fifteen. The other boy, whose name is not given, became so ill from shock at what they discovered that after a long illness he died.

They reached the old wych elm and, thinking this to be a good place to look for birds' nests, began their search. Robert climbed the tree and peered into the dense foliage. Suddenly he cried out in horror. His friends soon joined him. They climbed up the tree and peered down a hole that ran down the centre of the tree and which opened up into a natural cavity at the bottom. There at the bottom a face looked up at them, and to their horror they realised that it was a human skull.

Eventually, Professor Webster, a brilliant forensic expert, carried out his reconstruction of the skeleton and in his final report he indicated that this was a case of murder. From the professor's work the police were able to build up a reasonably accurate picture of the victim whose skeleton had been discovered in the hollow tree. She was a woman of between twenty-five and forty. Part of an outer garment was tightly pressed over the lower cavity of the jaw of the skull and stuffed into the cavity of the mouth. It was believed that this had been placed there before death and that the woman had suffocated in this way.

The hole at the top of the wych elm was only twenty-four inches in diameter and Professor Webster believed that she had been pushed into the hole before rigor mortis set in. The fact that there was evidence of clothing having been stuffed into her mouth pointed to murder and not suicide. According to the professor, the body had been in the tree about eighteen months, possibly longer.

After prolonged investigations it was assumed that the woman was a stranger to the area – but who was she and where did she come from? These questions may never be answered, but theories and possibilities are looked at in some detail in Mr McCormick's book and should the reader be interested in following the case, then I suggest that they read this unusually thorough and detailed account.

Dr Margaret Murray, an eminent archaeologist and a former Professor of Egyptology at London University, said this of the Hagley Wood murder:

'I believe that the dead woman here was another victim of the devil-worshippers. Like that of Walton (an old farm labourer who was murdered on St Valentine's Day, 1945) her body was found in an isolated place. I also believe that many of these murders with peculiar twists are the results of the activities of devil-worshippers.'

Mr McCormick, having read Dr Murray's works on witchcraft, was so impressed by her scholarship, her thoroughness and logical approach to such questions that he felt that she had discovered something of real value.

If it had been a normal case of murder by asphyxiation caused by the cloth stuffed into the woman's mouth, one would have thought that the whole of the corpse would have been stuffed into the hollow tree, but this was not the case. There was a bizarre feature about this crime, for some of the smaller bones of the skeleton were found buried at some distance from the tree. The fact that the finger bones were buried separately caused Dr Murray to believe this crime to be linked with witchcraft. In devil-worship the hand of an executed person was greatly coveted by the devotees of the cult. Dr Murray also insisted that there was evidence to show that devil-worship was practised in some remote parts of the Midlands.

Now, back to Miss Burnell and her dog Paddy. It was only a very short time after the dog's experience that the skeleton was discovered and it must be remembered that the dog had not acted in a strange manner either before or after the walks in Hagley Wood.

It is well known that dogs seem to have an uncanny perception of evil, especially where there is a reputed haunting. These animals have been literally frightened to death when they have been taken into haunted places.

It cannot be said with any certainty that Miss Burnell and her dog were anywhere near the tree in which the skeleton was discovered, as she was a stranger to the area and would not remember every detail of what she saw.

But the odd behaviour of the dog, quite uncharacteristic of the animal, leaves one thinking that possibly it knew that it was in the presence of something evil. According to Dr Murray, witch-craft was practised in remote parts of the Midlands. Could it be that Paddy sensed that here had been a ritual killing by someone under the influence of some evil force? There is no satisfactory conclusion, but the behaviour of the dog, the discovery of the skeleton soon afterwards and the subsequent revelations concerning a connection with witchcraft cannot rule out the fact that the influence of this wicked crime still lingered.